PR
2823
T9

19567

Twentieth century interpretations of Macbeth

TWENTIETH CENTURY INTERPRETATIONS
OF

MACBETH

A Collection of Critical Essays

Edited by
TERENCE HAWKES

Prentice-Hall, Inc. *Englewood Cliffs, N.J.*
A SPECTRUM BOOK

Library of Congress Cataloging in Publication Data
Main entry under title:

Twentieth century interpretations of Macbeth.

   (A Spectrum Book)
   Bibliography: p.
   CONTENTS: Hawkes, T. Introduction.—Spurgeon, C.F.E.
Shakespeare's imagery in Macbeth.—Murry, J. M. The time
has been. [etc.]
   1. Shakespeare, William, 1564-1616. Macbeth.
I. Hawkes, Terence.
PR2823.T9   822'.3'3   76-50914
ISBN 0-13-541458-X
ISBN 0-13-541441-5 pbk.

To Ann
and Dave
and Steve

10   9   8   7   6   5   4   3   2   1

PRENTICE-HALL INTERNATIONAL, INC., *London*
PRENTICE-HALL OF AUSTRALIA PTY. LIMITED, *Sydney*
PRENTICE-HALL OF CANADA, LTD., *Toronto*
PRENTICE-HALL OF INDIA PRIVATE LIMITED, *New Delhi*
PRENTICE-HALL OF JAPAN, INC., *Tokyo*
PRENTICE-HALL OF SOUTHEAST ASIA PTE. LTD., *Singapore*
WHITEHALL BOOKS LIMITED, *Wellington, New Zealand*

Contents

Introduction

by Terence Hawkes

When I strike a match, I perform one of the most distinctively "modern" of actions.

It is a modernity of various dimensions, both technological and symbolic. The household match and the safety match represent the fruits of a fairly sophisticated program of scientific research undertaken in the nineteenth century. And man's relationship with fire or light traditionally carries the notion of rebellion newly mounted against a prior, established order of things, as in the figures of Prometheus and Lucifer (both of these, incidentally, names appropriated by early match manufacturers). But the most fundamentally modern feature involved can perhaps be located elsewhere: in the fact that such an action replaces the series of complicated manual operations formerly required for the production of a flame by a single, simple motion of the hand. In this, striking a match shares the status of other quintessentially modern acts, such as pressing a button, pulling a trigger, moving a lever. It signals, in miniature, a process that might be said to manifest the essence of modern technology, and so of the modern world: the process of reduction.[1]

Macbeth has increasingly impressed twentieth century critics as a play with a peculiarly modern bearing. Despite its evident involvement with an older world, with witches, their incantations and their spells, those who have written about the play in our own time indicate a growing sense that its protagonist speaks with a modern voice, from within a modern political and moral situation, about modern matters. In the present collection of essays, therefore, from Caroline Spurgeon's recognition of a "Chaplinesque" quality in Macbeth (1935) and J. Middleton Murry's sense of his "new and terrible realm of experience" (1936), to Mary McCarthy's depiction of him as the "trepidant executive...modern and bourgeois" (1962) and D. J. Enright's placing of him as a prototype of the "hen-pecked husband" (1970) the theme

---

[1]The point is Walter Benjamin's: see Fredric Jameson, *Marxism and Form* (Princeton, N.J.: Princeton University Press, 1971), p. 75.

proves appropriately persistent. Clearly, *Macbeth* contains elements
that the twentieth century experience repeatedly recognizes and
responds to.

We might begin to account for this phenomenon by means of the
large, confirming observation that the play's date and place of composition, London 1605 to 1606, seem in general terms to locate it at the
beginning of that vast and complex process of economic, religious,
and political development in Western Europe from which the modern
world was to emerge. Much of *Macbeth's* hold on us possibly derives
from the oblique but penetrative insights it offers into the nature of
that world as judged by the standards of an older, yet still living
medieval one. And so, when Macbeth complains

> I have lived long enough. My way of life
> Is fall'n into the sear, the yellow leaf,
> And that which should accompany old age,
> As honour, love, obedience, troops of friends,
> I must not look to have; but in their stead,
> Curses not loud but deep, mouth-honour, breath,
> Which the poor heart would fain deny, and dare not.
>
> (V. iii. 22-28)

the general diagnosis this implies of the new world at its commencement
perhaps seems peculiarly apt to those who now sense its conclusion.
Macbeth witnesses a birth: we are in at the death.

But maybe we can also be more specific. On 5 November 1605 a
search by security forces, instituted at the personal behest of King
James, discovered beneath the Houses of Parliament a secret cache
containing enough gunpowder, fuses, and other implements to blow
the king, his ministers, and the lawful government of the entire state
sky-high.

It would be difficult to overestimate the shock this discovery gen-
erated amongst the population at large. The whole affair instantly
found itself raised to the level of trauma by the propaganda rapidly
instigated by James and his advisers and it quickly acquired dimensions resonant far beyond the immediate facts at issue. The event is
celebrated in Britain to this day with bonfires, fireworks, and the
burning in effigy of one of the conspirators. It was as if a new destructive, reductive age had begun—its dawn the light of the terrorist's
match.

Glynne Wickham has recently drawn attention to the extent of the
implications derived at the time from the Gunpowder Plot and its
discovery: in particular to the larger symbolic role James' own writings

and speeches carefully gave it.[2] It would of course be mistaken to argue that *Macbeth* in any sense takes the Plot as its direct subject: the relationship of great art to reality is rarely of that overt order. But it is not surprising that a play dealing explicitly with James' personal ancestry should contain at its core precise references to the trial of one of the alleged conspirators (in the Porter scene) or that the wider social, spiritual, and theological ramifications of the Plot—fully exploited by James in his pronouncements on the subject—should find themselves obliquely embodied in a play whose first performance (the evidence suggests) took place at Hampton Court in his presence and that of his guest King Christian IV of Denmark.[3]

In essence, the Plot's intent was, almost literally, shattering. Following Queen Elizabeth's death in 1603, James' accession to the throne in the same year had seemed to offer a solution to many of the problems facing England both at home and abroad. Moreover, it had seemed to hold out a specific promise in a particular case. James was already King James VI of Scotland. His presence on the throne of England seemed to presage the final, peaceful union of those two nations. As James VI and I in one person, he seemed to represent and literally to embody peaceful unity: that final knitting together of the peoples of England, Scotland, and Wales into a political and cultural identity whose imperial destiny was God-given and manifest, and for which the name "Great Britain" had recently been devised. The reunification of Britain, and the reunification of religion within Britain, stood as major items in the "scenario" of his reign that had been officially propagated. James was to be the second Brutus, destined to reunify the land founded by the first Brutus, and then riven by him in his folly. And it was that edifice of imminent unity that the Gunpowder Plot seemed designed to reduce to rubble. That the conspirators were foreign-backed Catholics, their confessions appeared to confirm. That they were also (and therefore) agents of the devil intent upon the destruction of God's divine plan for Great Britain and her people followed without question. Inspired by Lucifer, the conflagration they purposed had its analogue in the flames of Hell.

One of the central concerns of *Macbeth* is of course the disunity and disorder that the murder of King Duncan brings to Scotland. "Con-

[2]Glynne Wickham, "From Tragedy to Tragi-Comedy: *King Lear* as Prologue," *Shakespeare Survey* 26 (1973), pp. 33-48.

[3]Detailed information concerning *Macbeth's* relationship to the concrete events of its own day has been assembled and discussed at length by Henry N. Paul in his study *The Royal Play of Macbeth* (New York: The Macmillan Company, 1950). I am happy to acknowledge a considerable debt to this fascinating work.

fusion now hath made his masterpiece" (II, iii, 68), cries Macduff on discovering the body, and goes on to liken the carnage to "The great doom's image" (II, iii, 80). Moreover, the play proves quite explicit (and wholly in accord with the spirit of Elizabethan and Jacobean official pronouncements on the subject of political rebellion) in the connection it insistently forges between the actions of Macbeth and those of Lucifer. The figure of the former angel who, fallen from heaven, finds himself, in the words of Isaiah, "brought down to hell, to the sides of the pit" (Isaiah XIV, 12-15) clearly animates Malcolm's attempt to reassure Macduff by reminding him that, despite Macbeth's treachery, "Angels are bright still, though the brightest fell" (IV, iii, 22). The same scene is at pains to contrast the good works of the saintly English king whose touch ("Such sanctity hath heaven given his hand") is able miraculously to cure the sick, with the quite opposite handiwork of "Devilish Macbeth" (IV, iii, 117). In the event, the world brought about by this "devil" proves to be the location of what L. C. Knights calls "a particular kind of evil."

At its most fundamental level, the murder of Duncan results in the overthrow of a social structure based on principles of one sort, and its replacement by another structure based on principles of an opposite sort. Macbeth's crime violates, as he recognizes, the traditional "double trust" of loyalty and hospitality. He should

> against his murderer shut the door
> Not bear the knife myself.   (I. vii. 15-16)

After that violation, and because of it, the traditionally ordered society in which the guarantee of each man's position (even Macbeth's) resides in the monarch's own supremacy is replaced by a society in which the only guarantee seems to reside in the exercise of brute force. Disorder thus replaces order in a process whose mode demands the term "reductive." It manifests itself in minature in the banquet scene where Lady Macbeth's initial, rather nervous assertion of the traditional structure

> You know your own degrees, sit down   (III. iv. 1)

finds itself, after the appearance of Banquo's accusing ghost, reduced to

> Stand not upon the order of your going
> But go at once.   (III. iv. 120-121)

The qualities that originate in traditional social ordering, whose loss Macbeth later mourns as "honour, love, obedience, troops of friends"

(V, iii, 25) exit with the departing nobles. A new totalitarian tyranny replaces them.

The reduction involved is total, and every aspect of life reflects it. As Caroline Spurgeon points out, the play's imagery recurrently presents Scotland as sick, incapacitated, wholly diseased. But we may be more precise. It has often been remarked in the twentieth century that political corruption eventually takes its toll of the public currency of words themselves. The debased language of the Watergate conspiracy offers only the most recent example of a process whereby degeneration in the conduct of public affairs seems ineluctably to transmit itself to the language in which those affairs are conducted. In *Macbeth* at first, the ordered grandeur of Duncan's pronouncements reflects, and is reflected in, a stable, rooted society:

> Welcome hither.
> I have begun to plant thee, and will labour
> To make thee full of growing. Noble Banquo,
> That hast no less deserved, nor must be known
> No less to have done so, let me enfold thee
> And hold thee to my heart.   (I. iv. 27-32)

The rhythms, the phrases, the metaphors seem to embody an established and accepted scheme of values, a sense of an even-handed, just dispensation operating in human affairs, and an organic, authenticated harmony pertaining between humanity and the natural world. Macbeth's own early speeches overtly manifest similar values—indeed, positively reinforce them in an explicit affirmation of the analogical connection between Duncan's roles as king and father traditionally upheld in Jacobean society:

> Your Highness' part
> Is to receive our duties: and our duties
> Are to your throne and state children and servants;
> Which do but what they should, by doing everything
> Safe toward your love and honour.   (I. iv. 22-27)

But the change that overtakes such language after Duncan's murder is no less explicit. In a notable scene, Lady Macbeth's disjointed utterances indicate by their form as much as their content the absence of cohesion effected by the killing:

> Out, damned spot! Out, I say! One: Two: Why then 'tis time to do't.
> Hell is murky. Fie, my lord, fie! A soldier and afeard? What need

we fear who knows it, when none can call our pow'r to account? Yet
who would have thought the old man to have had so much blood in
him?   (V. i. 38ff

The model for such reduction presents itself right at the beginning
of the play in the language of those sources of evil whose influence on
Macbeth proves so dire. In its deliberate obfuscation, its ambiguity,
its concern to mislead rather than inform, the language of the Witches
demands that we judge it to be deliberately and fundamentally sub-
versive. It seeks to overturn that ordering of the world which every
society makes and, perceiving its own version as "natural," takes as
the basis of normality. "Fair is foul and foul is fair" aptly represents
its principal objective: the reversal of accepted values.

So committed a pursuit of disorder will inevitably involve language's
every aspect. For instance, forceful incantatory rhythms enable a new
and disturbing arrangement of nature to be asserted over an older ac-
credited one, so that otherwise random items, with no "natural" association, find themselves yoked together by a kind of prosodic violence
and thereby assigned a new and shocking status as "ingredients":

> Scale of dragon, tooth of wolf
> Witches mummy, maw and gulf
> Of the ravin'd salt-sea shark,
> Root of hemlock digged i' the dark,
> Liver of blaspheming Jew,
> Gall of goat, and slips of yew....   (IV. i. 22ff.)

When a cognate assertive process is applied in politics, it calls for a
cognate violence, generates a cognate degradation. So Macbeth's acceptance of the principles at stake in the Witches' language inevitably
leads to his acceptance of the principle of political murder. And the
reductive nature of that act mirrors and is mirrored by the decline in
language's confirming and communicative power, so powerfully illustrated first by the Witches, then by Lady Macbeth, and ultimately
by Macbeth himself. In short, when Macbeth murders the king, he also
murders the King's English.

Interestingly enough, the notion that violence done to the state will
inevitably also involve violence done to the language had recently
been confirmed for the audience of *Macbeth* by some of the evidence
presented at a well-known trial. The accused was a Jesuit priest, Father
Garnet: the issue, his implication in the Gunpowder Plot.

Kenneth Muir and F. L. Huntley have pointed out that in the spring
and summer of 1606 the case presented against Garnet had dwelt at

length on his use of verbal double-dealing, technically termed "equivocation," in his own defense.[4] Garnet's subsequent admission that he considered it perfectly acceptable to equivocate "if just necessity so require" had undoubtedly seemed outrageous to a society already disposed (and encouraged in this by its propaganda) to think the worst of Roman Catholic priests. As a result equivocation had rapidly and popularly become almost the badge of subversion.

It is important to realize that the question is not one of simple "lying." Equivocation of the type allegedly defended by Garnet's Jesuit order involved the deliberate and premeditated manipulation of language in order to obscure the truth and so, as it would appear to Shakespeare's audience, to strike at the foundations of the entire community. When that community is also by and large nonliterate, and thus dependent more than we can imagine on face-to-face colloquy as the repository of truth and certainty, the crime seems even more fundamental, able to effect the debasement of a whole way of life. In a theologically centered society it may readily be labeled devilish, and there is no doubt that much of the "hellish" quality of Macbeth's crime in this play derives from the extent to which, in his journey to damnation, he ultimately commits himself to those who reduce language in this way, and who may for that reason be justly described as

> juggling fiends...
> That palter with us in a double sense   (V. viii. 19-20)

It is against this background that, at the point in the play where the murder is about to be discovered, the Porter drunkenly presents himself as the guardian of the gate of Hell, and goes on to utter the allusions to Father Garnet which reinforce the metaphorical relationship between Macbeth's crime and that of the Gunpowder conspirators. Both warrant admission to Hell, and on the same terms:

> Faith, here's an equivocator, that could swear in both the scales against either scale; who committed treason enough for God's sake, yet could not equivocate to heaven. O, Come in equivocator. ...
> (II. iii. 10ff.)

In any community, language and way of life have an intricate connection. In *Macbeth*, the principle of equivocation can be seen to

[4]Kenneth Muir, Introduction to *Macbeth*, Arden ed. (London: Methuen & Co. Ltd., 1951), pp. xviii ff; and F. L. Huntley, *"Macbeth* and the Background of Jesuitical Equivocation," *PMLA*, 79 (1964), 390-99.

extend itself throughout the whole structure of a society in which all values are overturned. Thus, even so basic and important a distinction as that normally obtaining between men and women comes to acquire an equivocal dimension, becoming blurred and perverted by the crime and its perpetrators. Although nominally female, the Witches' sexual status appears immediately ambiguous to Banquo:

> You should be women,
> And yet your beards forbid me to interpret
> That you are so.   (I. iii. 45-47)

—and the response this authorizes in the audience appropriately constitutes an overturning of their conventional reaction to what then amounted to a feature of the contemporary stage. The convention that women's parts were taken by boy actors normally remains part of the "background" of the audience's response. Now, suddenly, by a direct reference to their sexual ambiguity, it assumes the status of "foreground." The same "overturning" motion can be sensed in Lady Macbeth's quite deliberate and ironic reference to her own sex:

> Come, you spirits
> That tend on mortal thoughts, unsex me here,...
> ...Come to my woman's breasts,
> And take my milk for gall...   (I. v. 37ff.)

—and later

> I have given suck, and know
> How tender 'tis to love the babe that milks me. ...   (I. vii. 54-55)

Here the boy actor's forceful references (and presumably gestures) to his/her anatomy stand the accepted practice on its head, and make Lady Macbeth's "womanliness" not just part of a passively accepted convention, but an almost embarrassingly active ingredient in the play's statement. It is one which requires her to function as a woman whose evil purposes demand that she abandon her female role as mother, and become a man.

The overturning is completed when Lady Macbeth, suitably "unsexed," finds herself matched by a Macbeth "quite unmann'd in folly" (III, iv, 74). Despite his protestations before the murder that

> I dare do all that may become a man;
> Who dares do more is none   (I. vii. 46-47)

and after it that

> What man dare, I dare   (III. iv. 99)

there can be little doubt that the drive to achieve the deed comes from Lady Macbeth, and that she quickly takes over the (then) traditionally assertive male role; one which reinforces her gibes at the, by comparison, "female" figure of her husband: "Are you a man?" (III, iv, 58) and, earlier,

> When you durst do it, then you were a man;
> And to be more than what you were, you would
> Be so much more the man.   (I. vii. 48-52)

Of course, as Cleanth Brooks and Eugene M. Waith point out, the "manliness" she urges on Macbeth involves a predictably reduced notion of what being "a man" means. Certainly her forceful suggestion that manliness lies in the act of murder (and his subsequent persuasion of Banquo's murderers in the same vein) indicates that the concept involved is a narrow one, capable of demolishing all scruples, of reducing all complexity to a single dimension, and by investing in simple physical strength and daring, of finding its aptest symbol in the bludgeon or the murderer's dagger. In a world where manliness of that reduced order holds sway, Lady Macbeth may be said to be well characterized by her husband's injunction:

> Bring forth men-children only;
> For thy undaunted mettle should compose
> Nothing but males.   (I. vii. 73-75)

However, as the play is at some pains to point out, when "manliness" is so diminished, its perpetrators cease to be men at all. By the end of the play, Macbeth has shrunk to the dimension of a mere beast: a "bear," a "hell-kite," a "hell-hound," and a "monster." Too late, he recognizes that the equivocal language that has seduced him has also reduced his manhood:

> Accursed be the tongue that tells me so,
> For it hath cowed my better part of man.   (V. viii. 16-17)

The reduction of man to the level of beast perhaps constitutes the final reduction that *Macbeth* chronicles so remorselessly, and it must rank as certainly the most terrible of degradations. From the moment of the murder to the end of the play, life increasingly ceases to hold any human significance or meaning for Macbeth. As always in Shakespeare, the victory over order turns out to be hollow. Only horrors abound and increase. Existence itself undergoes the final reduction to become a meaningless succession of hours and days:

> Tomorrow and tomorrow and tomorrow
> Creeps in this petty pace from day to day,

> To the last syllable of recorded time:
> And all our yesterdays have lighted fools
> The way to dusty death. Out, out, brief candle!   (V. v. 19-23)

Even drama, holding as ever a mirror up to nature, seems merely a metaphor of the same process:

> Life's but a walking shadow, a poor player
> That struts and frets his hour upon the stage
> And then is heard no more. It is a tale
> Told by an idiot, full of sound and fury,
> Signifying nothing.   (V. v. 24-28)

Of course, this represents Macbeth's view. A dramatist may be expected to account it only a measure of his degradation. Shakespeare's own conviction in the matter can be judged from the fact that when Macbeth's world has reached its final, fully reduced pitch, drama in effect redeems it. As John Holloway points out, the device that finally reverses the reductive process exploits an essentially "dramatic" mode in order to do so. The soldiers of Malcolm's avenging army proceed to "represent" Birnam Wood in an emblematic manner wholly germane to the nonrealistic stage on which the play itself takes place. In fact, with unity finally rehabilitated, the new king safely *en route* to his coronation, and James' ancestors amply restored thereby to the status which he, currently a member of the audience, inherits and embodies, the play's own "poor players" may be said to have been involved in concrete matters of some moment, with a continuity far outlasting their "hour upon the stage." As a result, *Macbeth* concludes by paying the living monarch a fine dramatic compliment.

But of course this constitutes only the climax of that series of insistent, oblique references to James which runs throughout *Macbeth* and marks one of its most distinctive features. The English king's healing touch described in Act IV, and said there to be passed on "to the succeeding royalty" (IV, iii, 155), unmistakably acknowledges James' own recent revival of the practice of "touching" for the King's Evil (scrofula); his continuing interest in witches meets an obvious response in a play that also confirms his own judgment, made in a learned study, *Daemonologie* (1597), that they were agents of the devil. By such glancing allusions, as well as others mentioned above, *Macbeth* ultimately seems almost to reach out and embrace the king in its action. As it does so, it may be said to redeem, by the vitality of that relationship with the living world, the sterile, reduced, and dead world of its protagonist. And the king and his royal guests, who began the performance as spectators, thus end it as participants.

Perhaps all great art requires the same transition. In any event, it represents a journey made in the opposite direction to Macbeth's, fulfilling not only a fundamental principle of drama traditionally said to be inscribed over the entrance to the Globe Theater, *Totus Mundus Agit Histrionem*, but also a more obviously political principle which Shakespeare evidently hoped, and James certainly claimed, should constitute the foundation of good government.

Of course, *Macbeth* is a tragedy and its implications reach far beyond the simple optimism that the compliment to James appears to suggest. Most modern critics agree that the play exhibits more concern with the diagnosis of evil in the modern world than with flattery of its royal audience. We may miss the purely "local" allusions, but Macbeth's reduced world, its language, its politics, are instantly familiar to us.

Yet that familiarity perhaps finally becomes the play's most complicating factor, making it difficult to "see" Macbeth as the self-damned wretch its structure demands. He looks too much like someone we know. His voice disconcertingly calls others, more recent and ordinary, to mind. His outlook, his way of life, share common features with our own. To condemn Macbeth, as the play invites us, is perhaps, ironically, to condemn much that makes us thrive.

On the other hand, history affords a no less ironic context for Shakespeare's overt assessment of James himself, Macbeth's opposite, as unifier and integrator. True, the state and his government survived the Gunpowder Plot. True, the unification with Scotland edged gradually forward, eventually to become a political reality. True, an entity called Britain emerged. True, it became Great in some senses and went on to fulfill an imperial destiny.

But within a generation, James' son and political heir had become the first European monarch to be deposed, tried, and executed by his own people in a shattering revolution. In fact, within a year of *Macbeth's* completion, other more slowly germinating seeds were being sown.

On 14 May 1607 Captain John Smith finally established the first permanent British settlement in North America. It was called Jamestown in honor of the monarch. Its plantations prospered. A dozen years later, the first systematic importation of African slaves to the colony had begun.

Also in 1607, two Irish earls, Tyrone and Tyrconnel, suddenly fled from Ireland to the Continent. Their lands accordingly became forfeit to the English Crown. Seizing the opportunity, James took the step of parcelling up that land and offering it for sale to Englishmen and Scotsmen prepared to move to Ireland. The colony thus created (it too was called a "plantation") would, it was hoped, provide a permanent "civilized" and Protestant bulwark against the native Catholic population and help, in the name of Christianity and the unity of Great Britain, to subdue it. The area involved is now called Ulster.

Other matches had been struck.

Shakespeare's Imagery in *Macbeth*

by Caroline F. E. Spurgeon

The imagery in *Macbeth* appears to me to be more rich and varied, more highly imaginative, more unapproachable by any other writer, than that of any other single play. It is particularly so, I think, in the continuous use made of the simplest, humblest, everyday things, drawn from the daily life in a small house, as a vehicle for sublime poetry. But that is beside our point here.

The ideas in the imagery are in themselves more imaginative, more subtle and complex than in other plays, and there are a greater number of them, interwoven the one with the other, recurring and repeating. There are at least four of these main ideas, and many subsidiary ones. One is the picture of Macbeth himself.

Few simple things—harmless in themselves—have such a curiously humiliating and degrading effect as the spectacle of a notably small man enveloped in a coat far too big for him. Comic actors know this well—Charlie Chaplin, for instance—and it is by means of this homely picture that Shakespeare shows us his imaginative view of the hero, and expresses the fact that the honours for which the murders were committed are, after all, of very little worth to him.

The idea constantly recurs that Macbeth's new honours sit ill upon him, like a loose and badly fitting garment, belonging to someone else. Macbeth himself first expresses it, quite early in the play, when, immediately following the first appearance of the witches and their prophecies, Ross arrives from the king, and greets him as thane of Cawdor, to which Macbeth quickly replies,

> The thane of Cawdor lives: why do you dress me
> In borrow'd robes?   (I. iii. 108)

And a few minutes later, when he is rapt in ambitious thoughts sug-

"Shakespeare's Imagery in Macbeth." From Caroline F. E. Spurgeon, *Shakespeare's Imagery and What It Tells Us* (New York: Cambridge University Press, 1935), pp. 324-35. Copyright © 1935 by Cambridge University Press. Reprinted by permission of the publisher.

gested by the confirmation of two out of the three "prophetic greet-
ings," Banquo, watching him, murmurs,

> New honours come upon him,
> Like our strange garments, cleave not to their mould
> But with the aid of use.   (I. iii. 144)

When Duncan is safely in the castle, Macbeth's better nature for a
moment asserts itself, and, in debate with himself, he revolts from the
contemplated deed for a threefold reason: because of its incalculable
results, the treachery of such action from one who is both kinsman and
host, and Duncan's own virtues and greatness as king.

When his wife joins him, his repugnance to the deed is as great, but
it is significant that he gives three quite different reasons for not
going ahead with it, reasons which he hopes may appeal to her, for he
knows the others would not. So he urges that he has been lately hon-
oured by the king, people think well of him, and therefore he should
reap the reward of these things at once, and not upset everything by
this murder which they have planned.

There is irony in the fact that to express the position he uses the
same metaphor of clothes:

> I have bought
> Golden opinions from all sorts of people,
> Which would be worn now in their newest gloss,
> Not cast aside so soon.   (I. vii. 32)

To which Lady Macbeth, quite unmoved, retorts contemptuously:

> Was the hope drunk
> Wherein you dress'd yourself?   (I. vii. 36)

After the murder, when Ross says he is going to Scone for Macbeth's
coronation, Macduff uses the same simile:

> Well, may you see things well done there: adieu!
> Lest our old robes sit easier than our new!   (II. iv. 37)

And, at the end, when the tyrant is at bay at Dunsinane, and the
English troops are advancing, the Scottish lords still have this image
in their minds. Caithness sees him as a man vainly trying to fasten a
large garment on him with too small a belt:

> He cannot buckle his distemper'd cause
> Within the belt of rule;   (V. ii. 15)

while Angus, in a similar image, vividly sums up the essence of what
they all have been thinking ever since Macbeth's accession to power:

> now does he feel his title
> Hang loose about him, like a giant's robe
> Upon a dwarfish thief.   (V. ii. 20)

This imaginative picture of a small, ignoble man encumbered and degraded by garments unsuited to him, should be put against the view emphasised by some critics (notably Coleridge and Bradley) of the likeness between Macbeth and Milton's Satan in grandeur and sublimity.

Undoubtedly Macbeth is built on great lines and in heroic proportions, with great possibilities—there could be no tragedy else. He is great, magnificently great, in courage, in passionate, indomitable ambition, in imagination and capacity to feel. But he could never be put beside, say Hamlet or Othello, in nobility of nature; and there *is* an aspect in which he is but a poor, vain, cruel, treacherous creature, snatching ruthlessly over the dead bodies of kinsman and friend at place and power he is utterly unfitted to possess. It is worth remembering that it is thus that Shakespeare, with his unshrinking clarity of vision, repeatedly *sees* him.

Another image or idea which runs through *Macbeth* is the reverberation of sound echoing over vast regions, even into the limitless spaces beyond the confines of the world. Echoing sound, as also reflected light, always interested Shakespeare; he is very quick to notice it, and in the earlier plays he records it often, quite simply and directly, as in the reverberating roll of drums in *King John,* the smack of Petruchio's kiss resounding through the church, Juliet's delicate picture of Echo with her airy tongue repeating "Romeo," Viola's assertion that were she Orsino, she would make the

> babbling gossip of the air
> Cry out "Olivia!"   (*Twelfth Night*, I. v. 283)

or her more fanciful remark to the duke that the tune he likes

> gives a very echo to the seat
> Where love is throned.   (II. iv. 21)

He specially loves, and describes repeatedly (in *A Midsummer Night's Dream, Titus Andronicus* and the *Taming of the Shrew),* the re-echoing sound of hounds and horn,

> the musical confusion
> Of hounds and echo in conjunction;
> (*Midsummer Night's Dream,* IV. i. 115)

its doubling and mocking quality attracts him:

> the babbling echo mocks the hounds,

> Replying shrilly to the well-tuned horns,
> As if a double hunt were heard at once;
>
>   (*Titus Andronicus,* II. iii. 17)

and it is this quality which Warwick applies most appositely when, having been roused in the small hours to soothe the sleepless and fretful king, he finally loses patience with Henry's fears that the revolutionaries must be fifty thousand strong, and retorts, somewhat tartly,

>   It cannot be, my lord;
> Rumour doth double, like the voice and echo,
> The numbers of the fear'd. Please it your grace
> To go to bed.   (*Henry IV, Part 2,* III. i. 96)

It is not until after 1600, and most noticeably in *Troilus and Cressida,* that Shakespeare uses this same idea of reverberation and reflection to illustrate subtle and philosophic thought. Ulysses' mind is full of it, and he applies it constantly; Kent, in *King Lear* (I, i, 155), seizes on an analogous natural fact to point the truth that noise and protestation do not necessarily indicate deep feeling; while in *Macbeth,* the peculiar quality of echoing and re-echoing sound is used to emphasise, in the most highly imaginative and impressive way, a thought constantly present with Shakespeare in his middle years, the incalculable and boundless effects of evil in the nature of one man.

Macbeth himself, like Hamlet, is fully conscious of how impossible it is to "trammel up the consequence" (I, vii, 3) of his deed, and by his magnificent images of angels pleading trumpet-tongued,

> And pity, like a naked, new-born babe,
> Striding the blast, or heaven's cherubin horsed
> Upon the sightless couriers of the air,   (I. vii. 21)

who

> Shall blow the horrid deed in every eye,
> That tears shall drown the wind,   (I. vii. 24)

he fills our imagination with the picture of its being broadcast through great spaces with reverberating sound.

This is taken up again by Macduff, when he cries,

>   each new morn
> New widows howl, new orphans cry, new sorrows
> Strike heaven on the face, that it resounds
> As if it felt with Scotland and yell'd out
> Like syllable of dolour;   (IV. iii. 4)

and again by Ross, when he is trying to break the terrible news of Macbeth's latest murders to Macduff—the destruction of his own wife and children—

> I have words
> That would be howl'd out in the desert air,
> Where hearing should not latch them.   (IV. iii. 193)

One can scarcely conceive a more vivid picture of the vastnesses of space than this, and of the overwhelming and unending nature of the consequences or reverberations of the evil deed.

Another constant idea in the play arises out of the symbolism that light stands for life, virtue, goodness; and darkness for evil and death. "Angels are bright" (IV, iii, 22), the witches are "secret, black and midnight hags" (IV, i, 48), and, as Dowden says, the movement of the whole play might be summed up in the words, "good things of day begin to droop and drowse" (III, ii, 52).

This is, of course, very obvious, but out of it develops the further thought which is assumed throughout, that the evil which is being done is so horrible that it would blast the sight to look on it; so that darkness, or partial blinding, is necessary to carry it out.

Like so much in the play it is ironic that it should be Duncan who first starts this simile, the idea of which turns into a leading motive in the tragedy. When he is conferring the new honour on his son, he is careful to say that others, kinsmen and thanes, will also be rewarded:

> signs of nobleness, like stars, shall shine
> On all deservers.   (I. iv. 41)

No sooner has the king spoken, than Macbeth realises that Malcolm, now a prince of the realm, is an added obstacle in his path, and suddenly, shrinking from the blazing horror of the murderous thought which follows, he cries to himself,

> Stars, hide your fires;
> Let not light see my black and deep desires.   (I. iv. 50)

From now on, the idea that only in darkness can such evil deeds be done is ever present with both Macbeth and his wife, as is seen in their two different and most characteristic invocations to darkness: her blood-curdling cry.

> Come, thick night,
> And pall thee in the dunnest smoke of hell,   (I. v. 51)

which takes added force when we hear later the poignant words. "She
has light by her continually" (V, i, 23); and his more gentle appeal in
the language of falconry,

> Come, seeling night,
> Scarf up the tender eye of pitiful day.   (III. ii. 46)

And when Banquo, sleepless, uneasy, with heart heavy as lead, crosses
the courtyard on the fateful night, with Fleance holding the flaring
torch before him, and, looking up to the dark sky, mutters,

> There's husbandry in heaven,
> Their candles are all out,   (II. i. 4)

we know the scene is set for treachery and murder.

So it is fitting that on the day following, "dark night strangles the
travelling lamp" (II, iv, 7), and

> darkness does the face of earth entomb,
> When living light should kiss it.   (II. iv. 9)

The idea of deeds which are too terrible for human eyes to look on is
also constant; Lady Macbeth scoffs it—"the sleeping and the dead,"
she argues, "are but as pictures" (II, ii, 53):

> 'tis the eye of childhood
> That fears a painted devil;

but Macduff, having seen the slain king, rushes out, and cries to
Lennox,

> Approach the chamber, and destroy your sight
> With a new Gorgon.   (II. iii. 76)

Macbeth boldly asserts he dare look on that "which might appal the
devil" (III, iv, 60), and the bitterness of defeat he realises on seeing
one "too like the spirit of Banquo" in the procession of kings, is expressed in his agonised cry,

> Thy crown does sear mine eye-balls;   (IV. i. 113)

while in his bitter and beautiful words at the close, the dominant
thoughts and images are the quenching of light and the empty reverberation of sound and fury, "signifying nothing" (V, v, 28).

The fourth of the chief symbolic ideas in the play is one which is
very constant with Shakespeare, and is to be found all through his
work, that sin is a disease—Scotland is sick.

So Macbeth, while repudiating physic for himself, turns to the doctor and says if he could, by analysis, find Scotland's disease

> And purge it to a sound and pristine health,
> I would applaud thee to the very echo.
> That should applaud again...
> What rhubarb, senna, or what purgative drug,
> Would scour these English hence?   (V. iii. 52)

Malcolm speaks of his country as weeping, bleeding and wounded, and later urges Macduff to

> make us medicines of our great revenge,
> To cure this deadly grief;   (IV. iii. 214)

while Caithness calls Malcolm himself the "medicine of the sickly weal," "the country's purge" (V, ii, 27). It is worth noting that all Macbeth's images of sickness are remedial or soothing in character: balm for a sore, sleep after fever, a purge, physic for pain, a "sweet oblivious antidote" (V, iii, 43); thus intensifying to the reader or audience his passionate and constant longing for well-being, rest, and, above all, peace of mind.

Other subsidiary motives in the imagery, which work in and out through the play, insensibly but deeply affect the reader's imagination. One of these is the idea of the *unnaturalness* of Macbeth's crime, that it is a convulsion of nature. This is brought out repeatedly and emphasised by imagery, as are also the terrible results of going against nature.

Macbeth himself says that Duncan's wounds

> look'd like a breach in nature
> For ruin's wasteful entrance,   (II. iii. 118)

and Macduff speaks of his murder as the sacrilege of breaking open the Lord's anointed temple (II, iii, 71). The events which accompany and follow it are terrible because unnatural; an owl kills a falcon, horses eat each other, the earth was feverous and did shake, day becomes night; all this, says the old man, is unnatural,

> Even like the deed that's done.   (II. iv. 10)

Macbeth's greatest trouble is the unnatural one that he has murdered sleep (II, ii, 36), and the whole feeling of dislocation is increased by such images as "let the frame of things disjoint" (III, ii, 16), or by Macbeth's conjuration to the witches with the terrible list of the con-

vulsions of nature which may result from their answering him. Indeed,
if from one angle the movement of the play may be summed up in
Macbeth's words,

> Good things of day begin to droop and drowse,   (III. ii. 52)

from another it is completely described by the doctor in his diagnosis
of the doomed queen's malady as "a great perturbation in nature"
(V, i, 10).

In addition to these running images symbolising or expressing an
idea, there are groups of others which might be called atmospheric in
their effect, that is, they raise or increase certain feelings and emotions.

Such is the action of rapid riding, which contributes and emphasises a
certain sense of rushing, relentless and goaded motion, of which we are
very conscious in the play. This is symbolised externally by the rapid
ride of the messenger to Lady Macbeth, arriving "almost dead for
breath," ahead of Macbeth, who himself has outridden Duncan (I, v, 37).
The king remarks in unconscious irony,

> he rides well,
> And his great love, sharp as his spur, hath holp him
> To his home before us.   (I. vi. 22)

It is noticeable what a large part riding plays in the images which
crowd on Macbeth's heated brain when he is weighing the *pros* and
cons of his plan (I, vii, 1-28): the new-born babe "striding the blast,"
heaven's cherubin horsed

> Upon the sightless couriers of the air,   (I. vii. 23)

and finally, the vision of his "intent," his aim, as a horse lacking sufficient spur to action, which melts into the picture of his ambition as a
rider vaulting into the saddle with such energy that it "o'erleaps itself," and falls on the further side.

The feeling of fear, horror and pain is increased by the constant and
recurring images of blood, these are very marked, and have been
noticed by others, especially by Bradley, the most terrible being Macbeth's description of himself wading in a river of blood, (III, iv, 136);
while the most stirring to the imagination, perhaps in the whole of
Shakespeare, is the picture of him gazing, rigid with horror, at his own
blood-stained hand and watching it dye the whole green ocean red
(II, ii, 60).

The images of animals also, nearly all predatory, unpleasant or
fierce, add to this same feeling; such are a nest of scorpions, a venom-
ous serpent and a snake, a "hell-kite" eating chickens, a devouring

vulture, a swarm of insects, a tiger, rhinoceros and bear, the tiny wren fighting the owl for the life of her young, small birds with the fear of the net, lime, pitfall or gin, used with such bitter ironic effect by Lady Macduff and her boy just before they are murdered, the shrieking owl, and the bear tied to a stake fighting savagely to the end.

Enough has been said, I think, to indicate how complex and varied is the symbolism in the imagery of *Macbeth,* and to make it clear that an appreciable part of the emotions we feel throughout of pity, fear and horror, is due to the subtle but definite and repeated action of this imagery upon our minds, of which, in our preoccupation with the main theme, we remain often largely unconscious.

The Time Has Been

by J. Middleton Murry

Perhaps the most marvellous moment in *Macbeth* is when the two actors suddenly emerge from their madness, and look upon their deed with the same naivety as we of the audience. Here again, as in *Hamlet,* though in a totally different fashion, the discrepancy between the character and the act is turned consciously to account. It becomes part of the consciousness which suffuses and animates the drama, as distinct from the consciousness aroused in the spectator by the drama. Suddenly, Macbeth and Lady Macbeth *see themselves,* with an absolute and terrible naivety. This power that is in them to see themselves, manifested as they manifest it, convinces us, as nothing else could now convince us, of their essential nobility of soul. And by this turn the situation becomes bottomless in profundity. That a man and woman should, in the very act of heinous and diabolical murder, reveal themselves as naive and innocent, convulses our morality and awakens in us thoughts beyond the reaches of our souls. So that it seems to us that the wonderful imagination of

> Pity, like a naked new-born babe,
> Striding the blast,

is embodied in the sudden birth of childlike astonishment in the eyes of the murderers themselves.

This links with all that has, so swiftly, gone before. The mystery of iniquity hath them in thrall. Whereas in *Othello,* the Tempter, "the common enemy of man," is a human agent in the drama, hating, contriving, entangling one not easily wrought, in *Macbeth* the weird sisters, of whom we catch no more than glimpses, do not hate or contrive or entangle. They merely reveal a future to him who will believe it.

Have they power over Macbeth or have they not? The question will not be answered by Shakespeare. He was sensitive to the *meaning* of

"The Time Has Been." From *Shakespeare* by J. Middleton Murry (London: The Society of Authors, 1936), Chapter XV, pp. 325-36. Copyright © 1936 by The Society of Authors. Reprinted by permission of The Society of Authors as the literary representatives of the Estate of John Middleton Murry.

the deep-rooted medieval belief that a man, by the aid of arts occult, might know some of the secrets of God; but the price exacted for this knowledge of the future was to sell one's soul to the Devil:

> Mine eternal jewel
> Given to the common enemy of man.   (III. i. 68)

But the superficial crudity of the profound medieval superstition disappears in *Macbeth*. Macbeth makes no bargain with the emissaries of the powers of darkness: nor are they bargainable. The knowledge offers itself to him: it is, indeed, as he says, "a supernatural soliciting." But he is not solicited to the treachery and murder which he commits. If it has been granted him to read a little in the book of destiny, and he has found its first sentence true, there is nothing that compels him to be assistant and accomplice to the working of the second.

> If chance will have me king, why, chance may crown me,
> Without my stir.   (I. iii. 144)

Why, then, does he "catch the nearest way"? Of course, on one level the answer is simple: "Because the play demands it. If Macbeth does not murder Duncan, there is no play." But neither is there a drama unless this act is made credible. How this is made credible is what concerns us.

Does Shakespeare mean us to believe that Lady Macbeth has read her lord aright between the lines of his letter when she declares that he "would not play false, but yet would wrongly win"? Perhaps. It does not matter. What he does mean us to believe, and makes us believe, is that, in a little while, under her influence, he is what she has read him to be. When Macbeth says:

> That but this blow
> Might be the be-all and the end-all here,
> But here, upon this bank and shoal of time,
> We'd jump the life to come—   (I. vii. 4-7)

not merely is he ready to risk a Hell, of whose reality the weird sisters were, though indirect, no trifling witnesses—which took some courage —but, more important, the murder of his king and guest is now to him, even if it was not before, "that which rather he does fear to do/ Than wishes should be undone." His soul has consented to the act.

It is the retribution in this life alone that Macbeth seems now to fear, and most the horror of the world of men at "the deep damnation" of Duncan's taking off. The murderer who will jump the judgment of the life to come, and all that it implies, needs but the hope that the murder will be unknown to do the deed. That hope will come: it will create itself. For the judgment of the life to come is projected conscience. Conscience once drugged, murder becomes but a matter of contrivance. And that is all. Macbeth is appalled not by the thought of the deed, but by the thought of failure to conceal it.

> *Macb.*   If we should fail?
> *Lady M*.   We fail!
>   But screw your courage to the sticking-place,
>   And we'll not fail.   (I. vii. 59-61)

She gives him all that he needs—the contrivance that the murder may be done, and hid. Hers has been the cool and fearless brain; hers the tense string to which his own is tuned. His sound accords:

>   Bring forth men-children only;
>   For thy undaunted mettle should compose
>   Nothing but males.   (I. vii. 72-74)

It is hard upon this that Shakespeare soars beyond sublunary achievement. The short scene which follows the murder is beyond criticism or comparison. It is a revelation—of depths hitherto quite hidden in the two accomplices. The first crack of the surface, the first glimpse beneath, comes with Lady Macbeth's:

>   Had he not resembled
>   My father as he slept, *I* had done't.   (II. ii. 13-14)

The second follows instantly when, as Macbeth enters with bloody hands, she cries—never before, never after, but only now—"My *husband!*"

These cracks are the more ominous, in that her surface had seemed the more steely. Suddenly, we know all that was concealed in her injunction, "to screw your courage to the sticking-place." To-day the phrase is current coinage, dull with use. The mind slides over it. But here, it starts out, quick with new life, as it was when Shakespeare first gave the words to Lady Macbeth. Then it was new; it was the first such metaphor in the English language. And as it was the first, so it is the greatest use of it. And what it meant, and means, is this:

   When you turn the little wooden screw on a violin—in those days it was a lute or a viol—to tighten a string, your fingers feel delicately for "the sticking-place," where the screw is tight and the string is taut; and you feel for it with a faint and subtle apprehension lest the string should snap. That is Shakespeare's figure and that is what Lady Macbeth has been doing to her soul, and by her example to her husband's. And her words: "Had he not resembled my father as he slept, *I* had done't," tell us that the screw has given way, or that the string has snapped.

The snapping of the strings. Almost we hear them go. The very words break sudden and abrupt.

> *Enter* Macbeth
>
> *Lady M.*   My husband!
> *Macb.* I have done the deed. Did'st thou not hear a noise?
> *Lady M.* I heard the owl scream and the crickets cry.
>   Did you not speak?
> *Macb.*   When?
> *Lady M.*   Now.
> *Macb.*   As I descended?
> *Lady M.* Ay!
> *Macb.* Hark!
>   Who lies i' the second chamber?
> *Lady M.*   Donalbain.
> *Macb.* This is a sorry sight. [*Looking on his hands.*]
> *Lady M.* A foolish thought, to say a sorry sight.   (II. ii. 15-21)

After the staccato dialogue, the weakness of that last line is wonderful. It is almost like a nursery rhyme. We see the pitiful and helpless smile. Then Macbeth begins to manifest the same amazing, terrible naivety which has taken possession of his wife. As with her, this naivety is not in his words alone, but in the very texture of the verse: like a child telling a ghost-story.

> *Macb.* There's one did laugh in's sleep, and one cried "Murder!"
>   That they did wake each other: I stood and heard them:
>   But they did say their prayers, and address'd them
>   Again to sleep.
> *Lady M.* There are two lodged together.

We hear the vacant laugh. Whose is the "foolish thought" now?

> *Macb.* One cried "God bless us!" and "Amen" the other;
>   As they had seen me with these hangman's hands.
>   Listening their fear, I could not say "Amen,"
>   When they did say "God bless us!"
> *Lady M.*   Consider it not so deeply
> *Macb. But wherefore could not I pronounce "Amen"?*
>   I had most need of blessing, and "Amen"
>   Stuck in my throat.
> *Lady M.*   These deeds must not be thought
>   After these ways; so, it will make us mad.   (II. ii. 22-34)

"After these ways" now, not "deeply" any more. At first, while she is fumbling for the broken string, to screw it tight again, she speaks at random: "Consider it not so deeply." But as she gathers control, she knows that he is not considering it deeply at all. He is considering it simply, and strangely, and fatally, as she also had been considering it. There is no word for that kind of contemplation, when two creatures, become themselves, look on the irremediable thing they did when they were not themselves. "Not after these ways," says Lady Macbeth—that is, "as we are doing now": that is, not deeply, but simply and terribly, with a child's staring eyes. "So, it will make us mad." And it does.

In that scene the contrast between character and act which is the necessary outcome of Shakespeare's method in tragedy, and the most peculiar feature of it, is taken up into the consciousness of the actors themselves; thereby it becomes dynamic in the process of the drama itself. It becomes (or is thenceforward felt by us to be) the hidden power which drives destiny to its conclusion. By it Macbeth and his wife are driven mad, in a totally new sense of madness. Whereas their former madness was a simple, though mysterious, becoming not-themselves; the new madness is the outcome of their effort to hold self and not-self together in one consciousness. It is what overtakes them in a new and terrible realm of experience which they have entered.

Shakespeare is not niggard of indications of the quality of this experience. The next major moment in the spiritual process of the drama is the appalling irony of Macbeth's words to Lennox and Ross:

> Had I but died an hour before this chance,
> I had liv'd a blessed time: for from this instant
> There's nothing serious in mortality:
> All is but toys: renown and grace is dead;
> The wine of life is drawn, and the mere lees
> Is left this vault to brag of.   (II. iii. 95-101)

The irony is appalling: for Macbeth must needs be conscious of the import of the words that come from him. He intends the monstrous hypocrisy of a conventional lament for Duncan; but as the words leave his lips they change their nature, and become a doom upon himself. He is become the instrument of "the equivocation of the fiend/ That lies like truth."

His "blessed time" is over: now the accursed time begins. There is a change in the nature of Time as he experiences it.

> *Macb.* Methought I heard a voice cry "Sleep no more!
> Macbeth does murder sleep," the innocent sleep,

> Sleep that knits up the ravell'd sleave of care,
> The death of each day's life, sore labour's bath,
> Balm of hurt minds, great nature's second course,
> Chief nourisher in life's feast,—
> *Lady M.*   What do you mean?
> *Macb.* Still it cried "Sleep no more!" to all the house:
> "Glamis hath murder'd sleep, and therefore Cawdor
> Shall sleep no more; Macbeth shall sleep no more."
>
>   (II. ii. 35-43)

Terrible words—infinitely terrible by the potency with which Shakespeare's strange art invests them. He clashes paradox against paradox to open the gulf between Macbeth's new condition of being and his former state. "Glamis hath murder'd sleep": we are straightway plunged into an abyss of metaphysical horror. He has murdered Sleep that is "the death of each day's life"—that daily death of Time which makes Time human. He has murdered that.

Now he and his wife are become like the tortured criminal of China, whose eyelids are cut away: but this not in the physical, but the metaphysical realm. Time is now incessant. Under the stress of this torture either the inward or the outward world must be shattered. The woman is driven the former way, the man the latter. She collapses, he endures. He now acts and speaks and utters, so far as it can be uttered, the consciousness of this condition:

> But let the frame of things disjoint, both the worlds suffer
> Ere we will eat our meal in fear and sleep
> In the affliction of these terrible dreams
> That shake us nightly: better be with the dead
> Whom we, to gain our peace, have sent to peace,
> Than on the torture of the mind to lie
> In restless ecstasy. Duncan is in his grave;
> After life's fitful fever *he* sleeps well...   (III. ii. 16-23)

From this condition there is no escape in death: he who has murdered Sleep has murdered Death also. He is the victim of uninterrupted and unending Time, chained to the wheel of an everlasting Now. "Better be with the dead," no doubt, if it were possible. But an impassable gulf now divides him from the possibility of what he means by Death. The only remedy is superhuman: to shatter the frame of things and make both the worlds suffer; to wrench the pin of human time out of the nave of the universe; to annihilate the distinction between Has Been and Is: to make all Time like his own.

By a simple phrase, which twice he puts in his lips, Shakespeare enforces upon our imagination Macbeth's dreadful experience of a change in the nature of time, a bottomless gulf dividing a blessed time from an accursed time, human time from inhuman time.

> *The time has been*
> That when the brains were out the man would die...
>
> (III. iv. 78-79)

> *The time has been* my senses would have cool'd
> To hear a night-shriek.   (V. v. 9-10)

And this sense of something strange that has happened to time itself, of Macbeth's having passed, across a bottomless and irremeable chasm, into a new time-medium, is gathered up and finally concentrated in the too-famous lines:

> *Macb.*   Wherefore was that cry?
> *Sey.* The queen, my lord, is dead.
> *Macb.*   She should have died hereafter
>   There would have been a time for such a word.
>   To-morrow, and to-morrow, and to-morrow
>   Creeps in this petty pace from day to day
>   To the last syllable of recorded time,
>   And all our yesterdays have lighted fools
>   The way to dusty death. Out, out, brief candle!
>   Life's but a walking shadow, a poor player
>   That struts and frets his hour upon the stage
>   And then is heard no more: it is a tale
>   Told by an idiot, full of sound and fury,
>   Signifying nothing.   (V. v. 15-28)

Too famous, we call these lines; because the context from which they derive their grim nuance of meaning is not lightly comprehended and too easily forgotten.

I do not profess to know exactly what the first five lines of Macbeth's speech mean; but I am certain that they do not mean what Dr. Johnson said they meant:

> Her death should have been deferred to some more peaceable hour; had she lived longer, there would have been a more convenient time for such a word, for such intelligence. Such is the condition of human life that we always think to-morrow will be happier than to-day.

Macbeth's meaning is stranger than that. "Hereafter," I think, is purposely vague. It does not mean "later"; but in a different mode of time from that in which Macbeth is imprisoned now. "Hereafter"—in the not-Now: *there* would have been a time for such a word as "the Queen is *dead.*" But the time in which he is caught is to-morrow, and to-morrow, and to-morrow—one infinite sameness, in which yesterdays have only lighted fools the way to dusty death. Life in this time is meaningless—a tale told by an idiot—and death also. For his wife's death to have meaning there needs some total change—a plunge across a new abyss into a Hereafter.

Perhaps I read too much into it; but it seems to me to be the inspired utterance of one "who lies upon the torture of the mind in restless ecstasy." It is the complete fulfilment of the terrible prophetic irony of Macbeth's words after the murder of Duncan:

> Had I but died an hour before this chance
> I had lived a blessed time; for from this instant
> There's nothing serious in mortality
> All is buy toys. ...   (II. iii. 95-99)

Then began the queer and sinister emphasis on "time": "the blessed time" is gone, an accursed time is come. And what an accursed Time may be, we glimpse in the speech: "She should have died hereafter." The blessed time does not appear very blessed to us—a time "that when the brains were out, the man would die," a time when Macbeth's senses "would have cool'd to hear a night-shriek." Nevertheless, that time was human. Now Macbeth knows what Keats called "the feel of not to feel it."

> The feel of not to feel it,
> When there is none to heal it,
> Nor numbed sense to steel it,
>   Was never said in rhyme.

Never completely, that is true: but never more nearly, or more mysteriously than in Macbeth's words.

"This dead butcher and his fiend-like queen," says Malcolm by way of epitaph upon them. But we know better. Neither butcher nor fiend are they, nor are they dead. They are creatures who, having murdered Sleep, have murdered Death. "And Death once dead, there's no more dying then."

The Demonic Metaphysics of *Macbeth*

by *Walter Clyde Curry*

In Shakespeare's time evil was considered to be both subjective and, so far as the human mind is concerned, a non-subjective reality; that is to say, evil manifested itself subjectively in the spirits of men and objectively in a metaphysical world whose existence depended in no degree upon the activities of the human mind. This objective realm of evil was not governed by mere vague and irrational forces; it was peopled and controlled by the malignant wills of intelligences—evil spirits, devils, demons, Satan—who had the ability to project their power into the workings of nature and to influence the human spirit. Such a system of evil was raised to the dignity of a science and a theology. The wisest of men—with the exception of a small minority who, like Bruno, sat in the seats of the Sadducees—believed in the world of evil spirits: Sir Matthew Hale, Bishop Hall, Richard Baxter, Dr. Henry More, Dr. Willis, Glanville, Lavater, Sir Thomas Browne, Catholics and Protestants alike, physicians, philosophers, theologians, Kings.[1] Even the scientist, Sir Francis Bacon, classifies knowledge of angels and unclean spirits under Natural Theology, and concludes:

> The same is to be understood of revolted or unclean spirits: conversation with them, or using their assistance, is unlawful: and much more in any manner to worship or adore them: but the contemplation and knowledge of their nature, power, and illusions, appears from Scripture, reason, and experience, to be no small part of spiritual wisdom.[2]

And that skeptic and militant Calvinist, Reginald Scot, while opposing the Sadducees on the one hand and the Neo-Platonists on the other, confesses with Augustine that these matters are above his capacity:

[1]Cf. E. E. Stoll, *Shakespearean Studies* (New York, 1927), p. 237.

[2]*The Advancement of Learning*, Bk. III, ch. ii, ed. Joseph Devy (London, 1904), p. 122.

> And yet so farre as Gods word teacheth me, I will not sticke to saie, that they are living creatures, ordeined to serve the estate, yet that they are the Lords ministers, and executioners of his wrath, to trie and tempt in this world, and to punish the reprobate in hell fier in the world to come.[3]

Since, then, this belief was so universal at the time, we may reasonably suppose that Shakespeare's Weird Sisters are intended to symbolize or represent the metaphysical world of evil spirits. Whether one considers them as human witches in league with the powers of darkness, or as actual demons in the form of witches, or as merely inanimate symbols, the power which they wield or represent or symbolize is ultimately demonic. Let us, therefore, exercise wisdom in the contemplation of the nature, power, and illusions of unclean spirits.

In the meantime, we may conveniently assume that in essence the Weird Sisters are demons or devils in the form of witches. At least their control over the primary elements of nature, the *rationes seminales*, would seem to indicate as much.[4] Why, then, should Shakespeare have chosen to present upon his stage these witch-likenesses rather than devils in devil-forms? Two equally valid reasons may be suggested. In the first place, the rather sublime devil and his angels of the earlier drama, opponents of God in the cosmic order and destroyers of men, had degenerated in the hands of later dramatists into mere comic figures; by Shakespeare's time folk conception[5] had apparently so dominated dramatic practice and tradition that cloven hoof, horns, and tail became associated in the popular imagination only with the ludicrous. As Whitmore says: "We thus see that devil-plays after *Faustus* progress steadily in the direction of comedy, a movement which reaches its logical conclusion in the monumental humours of Jonson's *The Devil is an Ass.*"[6] For Shakespeare's audience, therefore, the presentation of actual devils upon the stage could suggest only dimly, if at all, the terror and sublimity of a metaphysical world of evil. In the second place, witches had acquired no such comic associations. They were essentially tragic beings who, for the sake of certain abnormal powers, had sold themselves to the devil. As we have seen, everybody believed in them as channels through which the malignity of evil spirits might be visited upon human beings. Here, then,

---

[3]Reginald Scot, *Discoverie of Witchcraft*, ed. with *A Discourse of Devils and Spirits*, B. Nicholson (London, 1886) p. 453.

[4]See Chapter II [of Curry's book].

[5]E. K. Chambers, *The Medieval Stage* (Oxford, 1903), Vol. II, pp. 91, 147-48.

[6]C. E. Whitmore, *The Supernatural in Tragedy* (Cambridge, 1915), pp. 256, 263-66. Cf. Montague Summers, *The History of Witchcraft and Demonology* (London, 1926), pp. 276-312.

were terrifying figures, created by a contemporary public at the most intense moment of witchcraft delusion, which Shakespeare found ready to his hand. Accordingly he appropriately employed witch-figures as dramatic symbols, but the Weird Sisters are in reality demons, actual representatives of the world of darkness opposed to good....[7]

And finally, certain aspects of Lady Macbeth's experience indicate that she is possessed of demons. At least, in preparation for the coming of Duncan under her battlements, she calls upon precisely those metaphysical forces which have seemed to crown Macbeth. The murdering ministers whom she invokes for aid are described as being sightless substances, *i.e.*, not evil thoughts and "grim imaginings" but objective substantial forms, invisible bad angels, to whose activities may be attributed all the unnatural occurrences of nature. Whatever in the phenomenal world becomes beautiful in the exercise of its normal function is to them foul, and *vice versa;* they wait upon nature's mischief. She recognizes that they infest the filthy atmosphere of this world and the blackness of the lower regions; therefore she welcomes a night palled in the dunnest smoke of hell, so dense that not even heaven may pierce the blanket of the dark and behold her projected deed. Her prayer is apparently answered; with the coming of night her castle is, as we have seen, shrouded in just such a blackness as she desires. She knows also that these spiritual substances study eagerly the effects of mental activities upon the human body, waiting patiently for evidences of evil thought which will permit them entrance past the barriers of the human will into the body to possess it. They tend on mortal thoughts. For, says Cassian: "It is clear that unclean spirits cannot make their way into those bodies they are going to seize upon, in any other way than by first taking possession of their minds and thoughts."[8] Thus instead of guarding the workings of her mind against the assaults of wicked angels, Lady Macbeth deliberately wills that they subtly invade her body and so control it that the natural inclinations of the spirit toward goodness and compassion may be completely extirpated. Says she:

---

[7]Whitmore says: "Shakespeare avails himself of this universally held belief, and presents his Weird Sisters at first under the guise of witches....The Sisters do not derive their might from any covenant with the powers of evil, but are themselves such powers, owing their sinister capacities only to themselves," *op. cit.*, p. 256.

[8]John Cassian, *Conferences,* Vol. VII, ch. xxiv, in Henry Wace and Philip Schaff, eds., *A Select Library of Nicene and Post-Nicene Fathers,* New Series, Vol. XI (London, 1895), p. 371.

> Come you spirits,
> That tend on mortal thoughts, unsex me here,
> And fill me from the crown to the toe, top-full
> Of direst cruelty; make thick my blood,
> Stop up th'access and passage to remorse,
> That no compunctious visitings of nature
> Shake my fell purpose, nor keep peace between
> Th'effect and it. Come to my woman's breasts
> And take my milk for gall, you murth'ring ministers,
> Wherever, in your sightless substances,
> You wait on nature's mischief   (I. v. 45-55)

And without doubt these ministers of evil do actually take possession of her body even in accordance with her desire. As Mrs. Siddons remarks: "Having impiously delivered herself up to the excitements of hell, the pitifulness of heaven itself is withdrawn from her, and she is abandoned to the guidance of the demons whom she has invoked."[9]

Possession of Lady Macbeth's body enables these forces of evil to control her spirit. As Cassian says: "It is a fact that those men are more grievously and severely troubled who, while they seem to be very little affected by them in the body, are yet possessed in spirit in a far worse way, as they are entangled in their sins."[10] We must not imagine that this possession of spirit is accomplished by the infusion of the demonic substance in such a way that it actually penetrates the substance of the soul—only the spirit of God may be fused in this manner with the spirit of man. Rather the unclean spirits overwhelm the intellectual nature of man only when they are permitted to seize upon those members in which the vitality of the soul resides.[11] This is what happens to Lady Macbeth. The forces which take possession of her body do unsex her and fill her from crown to toe, top-full of direst cruelty; they thicken her blood and so stop up the passage to remorse. She becomes, for the most part, the fiend-like queen in thought and action.

[9]See Horace Howard Furness, ed., *Variorum edition of Macbeth* (Philadelphia, 1873), p. 473; for a description of Mrs. Siddons' acting of the part see *ibid.*, p. 303.

[10]*loc. cit.*, p. 371.

[11]Cassian, *loc. cit.*, p. 366.

The Naked Babe
and the Cloak of Manliness

by Cleanth Brooks

The debate about the proper limits of metaphor has perhaps never been carried on in so spirited a fashion as it has been within the last twenty-five years. The tendency has been to argue for a much wider extension of those limits than critics like Dr. Johnson, say, were willing to allow—one wider even than the Romantic poets were willing to allow. Indeed, some alarm has been expressed of late, in one quarter or another, lest John Donne's characteristic treatment of metaphor be taken as the type and norm, measured against which other poets must, of necessity, come off badly. Yet, on the whole, I think that it must be conceded that the debate on metaphor has been stimulating and illuminating—and not least so with reference to those poets who lie quite outside the tradition of metaphysical wit.

Since the "new criticism," so called, has tended to center around the rehabilitation of Donne, and the Donne tradition, the latter point, I believe, needs to be emphasized. Actually, it would be a poor rehabilitation which, if exalting Donne above all his fellow poets, in fact succeeded in leaving him quite as much isolated from the rest of them as he was before. What the new awareness of the importance of metaphor—if it is actually new, and if its character is really that of a freshened awareness—what this new awareness of metaphor results in when applied to poets other than Donne and his followers is therefore a matter of first importance. Shakespeare provides, of course, the supremely interesting case.

But there are some misapprehensions to be avoided at the outset. We tend to associate Donne with the self-conscious and witty figure— his comparison of the souls of the lovers to the two legs of the compass is the obvious example. Shakespeare's extended figures are elaborated in another fashion. They are, we are inclined to feel, spontaneous comparisons struck out in the heat of composition, and not carefully articulated, self-conscious conceits at all. Indeed, for the average reader the connection between spontaneity and seriously imaginative poetry is so strong that he will probably reject as preposterous any account of Shakespeare's poetry which sees an elaborate pattern in the imagery. He will reject it because to accept it means for him the assumption that the writer was not a fervent poet but a preternaturally cold and self-conscious monster.

Poems are certainly not made by formula and blueprint. One rightly holds suspect a critical interpretation that implies that they are. Shakespeare, we may be sure, was no such monster of calculation. But neither, for that matter, was Donne. Even in Donne's poetry, the elaborated and logically developed comparisons are outnumbered by the abrupt and succinct comparisons—by what T. S. Eliot has called the "telescoped conceits." Moreover, the extended comparisons themselves are frequently knit together in the sudden and apparently uncalculated fashion of the telescoped images; and if one examines the way in which the famous compass comparison is related to the rest of the poem in which it occurs, he may feel that even this elaborately "logical" figure was probably the result of a happy accident.

The truth of the matter is that we know very little of the various poets' methods of composition, and that what may seem to us the product of deliberate choice may well have been as "spontaneous" as anything else in the poem. Certainly, the general vigor of metaphor in the Elizabethan period—as testified to by pamphlets, sermons, and plays—should warn us against putting the literature of that period at the mercy of our own personal theories of poetic composition. In any case, we shall probably speculate to better advantage—if speculate we must—on the possible significant interrelations of image with image rather than on the possible amount of pen-biting which the interrelations may have cost the author.

I do not intend, however, to beg the case by oversimplifying the relation between Shakespeare's intricate figures and Donne's. There are most important differences; and, indeed, Shakespeare's very similarities to the witty poets will, for many readers, tell against the thesis proposed here. For those instances in which Shakespeare most obviously resembles the witty poets occur in the earlier plays or in *Venus and Adonis* and *The Rape of Lucrece;* and these we are inclined to dismiss as early experiments—trial pieces from the Shakespearean workshop. We demand, quite properly, instances from the great style of the later plays.

Still, we will do well not to forget the witty examples in the poems and earlier plays. They indicate that Shakespeare is in the beginning not too far removed from Donne, and that, for certain effects at least, he was willing to play with the witty comparison. Dr. Johnson, in teasing the metaphysical poets for their fanciful conceits on the subject of tears, might well have added instances from Shakespeare. One remembers, for example, from *Venus and Adonis:*

> O, how her eyes and tears did lend and borrow!
> Her eyes seen in her tears, tears in her eyes;
> Both crystals, where they view'd each other's sorrow. ...

Or, that more exquisite instance which Shakespeare, perhaps half-smiling, provided for the King in *Love's Labor's Lost:*

> So sweet a kiss the golden sun gives not
> To those fresh morning drops upon the rose,
> As thy eye-beams, when their fresh rays have smote
> The night of dew that on my cheeks down flows:
> Nor shines the silver moon one half so bright
> Through the transparent bosom of the deep,
> As does thy face through tears of mine give light:
> Thou shin'st in every tear that I do weep,
> No drop but as a coach doth carry thee:
> So ridest thou triumphing in my woe.
> Do but behold the tears that swell in me,
> And they thy glory through my grief will show:
> But do not love thyself — then thou wilt keep
> My tears for glasses, and still make me weep.

But Berowne, we know, at the end of the play, foreswears all such

> Taffeta phrases, silken terms precise,
> Three-piled hyperboles, spruce affectation,
> Figures pedantical...

in favor of "russet yeas and honest kersey noes." It is sometimes assumed that Shakespeare did the same thing in his later dramas, and certainly the epithet "taffeta phrases" does not describe the great style of *Macbeth* and *Lear.* Theirs is assuredly of a tougher fabric. But "russet" and "honest kersey" do not describe it either. The weaving was not so simple as that.

The weaving was very intricate indeed—if anything, *more* rather than *less* intricate than that of *Venus and Adonis*, though obviously the pattern was fashioned in accordance with other designs, and yielded other kinds of poetry. But in suggesting that there is a real continuity between the imagery of *Venus and Adonis,* say, and that of a play like *Macbeth,* I am glad to be able to avail myself of Coleridge's support. I refer to the remarkable fifteenth chapter of the *Biographia.*

There Coleridge stresses not the beautiful tapestry-work—the purely visual effect—of the images, but quite another quality. He suggests that Shakespeare was prompted by a secret dramatic instinct to realize, in the imagery itself, that "constant intervention and running comment by tone, look and gesture" ordinarily provided by the actor, and that Shakespeare's imagery becomes under this prompting "a series and never broken chain...always vivid and, because unbroken, often minute. ..." Coleridge goes on, a few sentences later, to emphasize further "the perpetual activity of attention required on the part of the reader, ...the rapid flow, the quick change, and the playful nature of the thoughts and images."

These characteristics, Coleridge hastens to say, are not in themselves enough to make superlative poetry. "They become proofs of original genius only as far as they are modified by a predominant passion; or by associated thoughts or images awakened by that passion; or when they have the effect of reducing multitude to unity, or succession to an instant; or lastly, when a human and intellectual life is transferred to them from the poet's own spirit."

Of the intellectual vigor which Shakespeare possessed, Coleridge then proceeds to speak—perhaps extravagantly. But he goes on to say: "In Shakespeare's *poems,* the creative power and the intellectual energy wrestle as in a war embrace. Each in its excess of strength seems to threaten the extinction of the other."

I am tempted to gloss Coleridge's comment here, perhaps too heavily, with remarks taken from Chapter XIII where he discusses the distinction between the Imagination and the Fancy—the modifying and creative power, on the one hand, and on the other, that "mode of Memory"..."blended with, and modified by...Choice." But if in *Venus and Adonis* and *The Rape of Lucrece* the powers grapple "in a war embrace," Coleridge goes on to pronounce: "At length, in the *Drama* they were reconciled, and fought each with its shield before the breast of the other."

It is a noble metaphor. I believe that it is also an accurate one, and that it comprises one of the most brilliant insights ever made into the nature of the dramatic poetry of Shakespeare's mature style. If it is accurate, we shall expect to find, even in the mature poetry, the "never broken chain" of images, "always vivid and, because unbroken, often minute," but we shall expect to find the individual images, not me-

chanically linked together in the mode of Fancy, but organically related, modified by "a predominant passion," and mutually modifying
each other.

T. S. Eliot has remarked that "The difference between imagination
and fancy, in view of [the] poetry of wit, is a very narrow one." If I
have interpreted Coleridge correctly, he is saying that in Shakespeare's greatest work, the distinction lapses altogether—or rather,
that one is caught up and merged in the other. As his latest champion,
I. A. Richards, observes: "Coleridge often insisted—and would have
insisted still more often had he been a better judge of his reader's
capacity for misunderstanding—that Fancy and Imagination are not
exclusive of, or inimical to, one another."

I began by suggesting that our reading of Donne might contribute
something to our reading of Shakespeare, though I tried to make plain
the fact that I had no design of trying to turn Shakespeare into Donne,
or—what I regard as nonsense—of trying to exalt Donne above Shakespeare. I have in mind specifically some such matter as this: that
since the *Songs and Sonets* of Donne, no less than *Venus and Adonis,*
requires a "perpetual activity of attention...on the part of the reader
from the rapid flow, the quick change, and the playful nature of the
thoughts and images," the discipline gained from reading Donne may
allow us to see more clearly the survival of such qualities in the later
style of Shakespeare. And, again, I have in mind some such matter
as this: that if a reading of Donne has taught us that the "rapid flow,
the quick change, and the playful nature of the thoughts and images"
—qualities which we are all too prone to associate merely with the
fancy—can, on occasion, take on imaginative power, we may, thus
taught, better appreciate details in Shakespeare which we shall otherwise dismiss as merely fanciful, or, what is more likely, which we
shall simply ignore altogether.

With Donne, of course, the chains of imagery, "always vivid" and
"often minute" are perfectly evident. For many readers they are all
too evident. The difficulty is not to prove that they exist, but that,
on occasion, they may subserve a more imaginative unity. With
Shakespeare, the difficulty may well be to prove that the chains exist
at all. In general, we may say, Shakespeare has made it relatively
easy for his admirers to choose what they like and neglect what they
like. What he gives on one or another level is usually so magnificent
that the reader finds it easy to ignore other levels.

Yet there are passages not easy to ignore and on which even critics
with the conventional interests have been forced to comment. One of
these passages occurs in *Macbeth,* Act I, Scene vii, where Macbeth
compares the pity for his victim-to-be, Duncan, to

> a naked new-born babe,
> Striding the blast, or heaven's cherubim, hors'd
> Upon the sightless couriers of the air....

The comparison is odd, to say the least. Is the babe natural or super-natural—an ordinary, helpless baby, who, as newborn, could not, of course, even toddle, much less stride the blast? Or is it some infant Hercules, quite capable of striding the blast, but, since it is powerful and not helpless, hardly the typical pitiable object?

Shakespeare seems bent upon having it both ways—and, if we read on through the passage—bent upon having the best of both worlds; for he proceeds to give us the option: pity is like the babe "or heaven's cherubim" who quite appropriately, of course, do ride the blast. Yet, even if we waive the question of the legitimacy of the alternative (of which Shakespeare so promptly avails himself), is the cherubim comparison really any more successful than is the babe comparison? Would not one of the great warrior archangels be more appropriate to the scene than the cherub? Does Shakespeare mean for pity or for fear of retribution to be dominant in Macbeth's mind?

Or is it possible that Shakespeare could not make up his own mind? Was he merely writing hastily and loosely, and letting the word "pity" suggest the typically pitiable object, the babe naked in the blast, and then, stirred by the vague notion that some threat to Macbeth should be hinted, using "heaven's cherubim"—already suggested by "babe"— to convey the hint? Is the passage vague or precise? Loosely or tightly organized? Comments upon the passage have ranged all the way from one critic's calling it "pure rant, and intended to be so" to another's laudation: "Either like a mortal babe, terrible in helplessness; or like heaven's angel-children, mighty in love and compassion. This magnificent passage. ...

An even more interesting, and perhaps more disturbing passage in the play is that in which Macbeth describes his discovery of the murder:

> Here lay Duncan,
> His silver skin lac'd with his golden blood;
> And his gash'd stabs, look'd like a breach in nature
> For ruin's wasteful entrance: there, the murderers,
> Steep'd in the colours of their trade, their daggers
> Unmannerly breech'd with gore. ...

It is amusing to watch the textual critics, particularly those of the eighteenth century, fight a stubborn rear-guard action against the acceptance of "breech'd." Warburton emended "breech'd" to "reech'd"; Johnson, to "drench'd"; Seward, to "hatch'd." Other critics argued that the *breeches* implied were really the handles of the daggers, and that, accordingly, "breech'd" actually here meant "sheathed." The Variorum page witnesses the desperate character of the defense, but the position has had to be yielded, after all. *The Shakespeare Glossary* defines "breech'd" as meaning "covered as with breeches," and thus leaves the poet committed to a reading which must still shock the average reader as much as it shocked that nineteenth-century critic who pronounced upon it as follows: "A metaphor must not be far-fetched nor dwell upon the details of a disgusting picture, as in these lines. There is little, and that far-fetched, similarity between *gold lace* and *blood,* or between *bloody daggers* and *breech'd legs.* The slight-ness of the similarity, recalling the greatness of the dissimilarity, disgusts us with the attempted comparison."

The two passages are not of the utmost importance, I dare say, though the speeches (of which each is a part) are put in Macbeth's mouth and come at moments of great dramatic tension in the play. Yet, in neither case is there any warrant for thinking that Shakespeare was not trying to write as well as he could. Moreover, whether we like it or not, the imagery is fairly typical of Shakespeare's mature style. Either passage ought to raise some qualms among those who retreat to Shakespeare's authority when they seek to urge the claims of "noble simplicity." They are hardly simple. Yet it is possible that such pas-sages as these may illustrate another poetic resource, another type of imagery which, even in spite of its apparent violence and complication, Shakespeare could absorb into the total structure of his work.

Shakespeare, I repeat, is not Donne—is a much greater poet than Donne; yet the example of his typical handling of imagery will scarce-ly render support to the usual attacks on Donne's imagery—for, with regard to the two passages in question, the second one, at any rate, is about as strained as Donne is at his most extreme pitch.

Yet I think that Shakespeare's daggers attired in their bloody breeches can be defended as poetry, and as characteristically Shakespearean poetry. Furthermore, both this passage and that about the newborn babe, it seems to me, are far more than excrescences, mere extrava-gances of detail: each, it seems to me, contains a central symbol of the play, and symbols which we must understand if we are to understand either the detailed passage or the play as a whole.

If this be true, then more is at stake than the merit of the quoted lines taken as lines. (The lines as constituting mere details of a larger structure could, of course, be omitted in the acting of the play with-out seriously damaging the total effect of the tragedy—though this argument obviously cuts two ways. Whole scenes, and admittedly fine scenes, might also be omitted—have in fact *been* omitted—without quite destroying the massive structure of the tragedy.) What is at stake is the whole matter of the relation of Shakespeare's imagery to the total structures of the plays themselves.

I should like to use the passages as convenient points of entry into the larger symbols which dominate the play. They *are* convenient because, even if we judge them to be faulty, they demonstrate how obsessive for Shakespeare the symbols were—they demonstrate how far the conscious (or unconscious) symbolism could take him.

If we see how the passages are related to these symbols, and they to the tragedy as a whole, the main matter is achieved; and having seen this, if we still prefer "to wish the lines away," that, of course, is our privilege. In the meantime, we may have learned something about Shakespeare's methods—not merely of building metaphors—but of encompassing his larger meanings.

One of the most startling things which has come out of Miss Spurgeon's book on Shakespeare's imagery is her discovery of the "old clothes" imagery in *Macbeth*. As she points out: "The idea constantly recurs that Macbeth's new honours sit ill upon him, like a loose and badly fitting garment, belonging to someone else." And she goes on to quote passage after passage in which the idea is expressed. But, though we are all in Miss Spurgeon's debt for having pointed this out, one has to observe that Miss Spurgeon has hardly explored the full implications of her discovery. Perhaps her interest in classifying and cataloguing the imagery of the plays has obscured for her some of the larger and more important relationships. At any rate, for reasons to be given below, she has realized only a part of the potentialities of her discovery.

Her comment on the clothes imagery reaches its climax with the following paragraphs:

> And, at the end, when the tyrant is at bay at Dunsinane, and the English troops are advancing, the Scottish lords still have this image in their minds. Caithness sees him as a man vainly trying to fasten a large garment on him with too small a belt:
>
> > He cannot buckle his distemper'd cause
> > Within the belt of rule;
>
> while Angus, in a similar image, vividly sums up the essence of what they all have been thinking ever since Macbeth's accession to power:
>
> > now does he feel his title
> > Hang loose about him, like a giant's robe
> > Upon a dwarfish thief.

This imaginative picture of a small, ignoble man encumbered and degraded by garments unsuited to him, should be put against the view emphasized by some critics (notably Coleridge and Bradley) of the likeness between Macbeth and Milton's Satan in grandeur and sublimity.

Undoubtedly Macbeth…is great, magnificently great…But he could never be put beside, say, Hamlet or Othello, in nobility of nature; and there *is* an aspect in which he is but a poor, vain, cruel, treacherous creature, snatching ruthlessly over the dead bodies of kinsman and friend at place and power he is utterly unfitted to possess. It is worth remembering that it is thus that Shakespeare, with his unshrinking clarity of vision, repeatedly *sees* him.

But this is to make primary what is only one aspect of the old-clothes imagery! And there is no warrant for interpreting the garment imagery as used by Macbeth's enemies, Caithness and Angus, to mean that *Shakespeare* sees Macbeth as a poor and somewhat comic figure.

The crucial point of the comparison, it seems to me, lies not in the smallness of the man and the largeness of the robes, but rather in the fact that—whether the man be large or small—these are not *his* garments; in Macbeth's case they are actually stolen garments. Macbeth is uncomfortable in them because he is continually conscious of the fact that they do not belong to him. There is a further point, and it is one of the utmost importance; the oldest symbol for the hypocrite is that of the man who cloaks his true nature under a disguise. Macbeth loathes playing the part of the hypocrite—and actually does not play it too well. If we keep this in mind as we look back at the instances of the garment images which Miss Spurgeon has collected for us, we shall see that the pattern of imagery becomes very rich indeed. Macbeth says in Act I:

> The Thane of Cawdor lives: why do you dress me
> In borrow'd robes?

Macbeth at this point wants no honors that are not honestly his. Banquo says in Act I:

> New honours come upon him,
> Like our strange garments, cleave not to their mould,
> But with the aid of use.

But Banquo's remark, one must observe, is not censorious. It is indeed a compliment to say of one that he wears new honors with some awkwardness. The observation becomes ironical only in terms of what is to occur later.

Macbeth says in Act I:

> He hath honour'd me of late; and I have bought
> Golden opinions from all sorts of people,
> Which would be worn now in their newest gloss,
> Not cast aside so soon.

Macbeth here is proud of his new clothes: he is happy to wear what he has truly earned. It is the part of simple good husbandry not to throw aside these new garments and replace them with robes stolen from Duncan.

But Macbeth has already been wearing Duncan's garments in anticipation, as his wife implies in the metaphor with which she answers him:

> Was the hope drunk,
> Wherein you dress'd yourself?

(The metaphor may seem hopelessly mixed, and a full and accurate analysis of such mixed metaphors in terms of the premises of Shakespeare's style waits upon some critic who will have to consider not only this passage but many more like it in Shakespeare.) For our purposes here, however, one may observe that the psychological line, the line of the basic symbolism, runs on unbroken. A man dressed in a drunken hope is garbed in strange attire indeed—a ridiculous dress which accords thoroughly with the contemptuous picture that Lady Macbeth wishes to evoke. Macbeth's earlier dream of glory has been a drunken fantasy merely, if he flinches from action now.

But the series of garment metaphors which run through the play is paralleled by a series of masking or cloaking images which—if we free ourselves of Miss Spurgeon's rather mechanical scheme of classification—show themselves to be merely variants of the garments which hide none too well his disgraceful self. He is consciously hiding that self throughout the play.

"False face must hide what the false heart doth know," he counsels Lady Macbeth before the murder of Duncan; and later, just before the murder of Banquo, he invokes night to "scarf up the eye of pitiful day."

One of the most powerful of these cloaking images is given to Lady Macbeth in the famous speech in Act I:

> Come, thick night,
> And pall thee in the dunnest smoke of hell,
> That my keen knife see not the wound it makes,

> Nor heaven peep through the blanket of the dark,
> To cry, "Hold, Hold!"

I suppose that it is natural to conceive the "keen knife" here as held in her own hand. Lady Macbeth is capable of wielding it. And in this interpretation, the imagery is thoroughly significant. Night is to be doubly black so that not even her knife may see the wound it makes. But I think that there is good warrant for regarding her "keen knife" as Macbeth himself. She has just, a few lines above, given her analysis of Macbeth's character as one who would "not play false,/ And yet [would]wrongly win." To bring him to the point of action, she will have to "chastise [him] with the valour of [her] tongue." There is good reason, then, for her to invoke night to become blacker still— to pall itself in the "dunnest smoke of hell." For night must not only screen the deed from the eye of heaven—conceal it at least until it is too late for heaven to call out to Macbeth "Hold, Hold!" Lady Macbeth would have night blanket the deed from the hesitant doer. The imagery thus repeats and reinforces the substance of Macbeth's anguished aside uttered in the preceding scene:

> Let not light see my black and deep desires;
> The eye wink at the hand; yet let that be
> Which the eye fears, when it is done, to see.

I do not know whether "blanket" and "pall" qualify as garment metaphors in Miss Spurgeon's classification: yet one is the clothing of sleep, and the other, the clothing of death—they are the appropriate garments of night; and they carry on an important aspect of the general clothes imagery. It is not necessary to attempt to give here an exhaustive list of instances of the garment metaphor; but one should say a word about the remarkable passage in II, iii.

Here, after the discovery of Duncan's murder, Banquo says

> And when we have our naked frailties hid,
> That suffer in exposure, let us meet,
> And question this most bloody piece of work—

that is, "When we have clothed ourselves against the chill morning air, let us meet to discuss this bloody piece of work." Macbeth answers, as if his subconscious mind were already taking Banquo's innocent phrase, "naked frailities," in a deeper, ironic sense:

> Let's briefly put on manly readiness....

It is ironic; for the "manly readiness" which he urges the other lords to put on, is, in his own case, a hypocrite's garment: he can only pretend to be the loyal, grief-striken liege who is almost unstrung by the horror of Duncan's murder.

But the word "manly" carries still a further ironic implication: earlier, Macbeth had told Lady Macbeth that he dared

> do all that may become a man;
> Who dares do more is none.

Under the weight of her reproaches of cowardice, however, he *has* dared do more, and has become less than a man, a beast. He has already laid aside, therefore, one kind of "manly readiness" and has assumed another: he has garbed himself in a sterner composure than that which he counsels to his fellows—the hard and inhuman "manly readiness" of the resolved murderer.

The clothes imagery, used sometimes with emphasis on one aspect of it, sometimes on another, does pervade the play. And it should be evident that the daggers "breech'd with gore"—though Miss Spurgeon does not include the passage in her examples of clothes imagery— represent one more variant of this general symbol. Consider the passage once more:

> Here lay Duncan,
> His silver skin lac'd with his golden blood;
> And his gash'd stabs look'd like a breach in nature
> For ruin's wasteful entrance: there, the murderers,
> Steep'd in the colours of their trade, their daggers
> Unmannerly breech'd with gore....

The clothes imagery runs throughout the passage; the body of the king is dressed in the most precious of garments, the blood royal itself; and the daggers too are dressed—in the same garment. The daggers, "naked" except for their lower parts which are reddened with blood, are like men in "unmannerly" dress—men, naked except for their red breeches, lying beside the red-handed grooms. The figure, though vivid, is fantastic; granted. But the basis for the comparison is *not* slight and adventitious. The metaphor fits the real situation on the deepest levels. As Macbeth and Lennox burst into the room, they find the daggers wearing, as Macbeth knows all too well, a horrible masquerade. They have been carefully "clothed" to play a part. They are not honest daggers, honorably naked in readiness to guard the king, or "mannerly" clothed in their own sheaths. Yet the disguise which they wear will enable Macbeth to assume the robes of Duncan—robes to which he is no more entitled than are the daggers to the royal garments which they now wear, grotesquely.

The reader will, of course, make up his own mind as to the value of the passage. But the metaphor in question, in the light of the other garment imagery, cannot be dismissed as merely a strained ingenuity, irrelevant to the play. And the reader who *does* accept it as poetry will probably be that reader who knows the play best, not the reader who knows it slightly and regards Shakespeare's poetry as a rhetoric more or less loosely draped over the "content" of the play.

And now what can be said of pity, the "naked newborn babe"? Though Miss Spurgeon does not note it (since the governing scheme of her book would have hardly allowed her to see it), there are, by the way, a great many references to babes in this play—references which occur on a number of levels. The babe appears sometimes as a character, such as Macduff's child; sometimes as a symbol, like the crowned babe and the bloody babe which are raised by the witches on the occasion of Macbeth's visit to them; sometimes, in a metaphor, as in the passage under discussion. The number of such references can hardly be accidental; and the babe turns out to be, as a matter of fact, perhaps the most powerful symbol in the tragedy.

But to see this fully, it will be necessary to review the motivation of the play. The stimulus to Duncan's murder, as we know, was the prophecy of the Weird Sisters. But Macbeth's subsequent career of bloodshed stems from the same prophecy. Macbeth was to have the crown, but the crown was to pass to Banquo's children. The second part of the prophecy troubles Macbeth from the start. It does not oppress him, however, until the crown has been won. But from this point on, the effect of the prophecy is to hurry Macbeth into action and more action until he is finally precipitated into ruin.

We need not spend much time in speculating on whether Macbeth, had he been content with Duncan's murder, had he tempted fate no further, had he been willing to court the favor of his nobles, might not have died peaceably in bed. We are dealing, not with history, but with a play. Yet, even in history the usurper sometimes succeeds; and he sometimes succeeds on the stage. Shakespeare himself knew of, and wrote plays about, usurpers who successfully maintained possession of the crown. But, in any case, this much is plain: the train of murders into which Macbeth launches aggravates suspicions of his guilt and alienates the nobles.

Yet, a Macbeth who could act once, and then settle down to enjoy the fruits of this one attempt to meddle with the future would, of course, not be Macbeth. For it is not merely his great imagination and his warrior courage in defeat which redeem him for tragedy and place him beside the other great tragic protagonists: rather, it is his attempt to conquer the future, an attempt involving him, like Oedipus, in a desperate struggle with fate itself. It is this which holds our imaginative sympathy, even after he has degenerated into a bloody tyrant and has become the slayer of Macduff's wife and children.

To sum up, there can be no question that Macbeth stands at the height of his power after his murder of Duncan, and that the plan — as outlined by Lady Macbeth — has been relatively successful. The road turns toward disaster only when Macbeth decides to murder Banquo. Why does he make this decision? Shakespeare has pointed up the basic motivation very carefully:

> Then prophet-like,
> They hail'd him father to a line of kings.
> Upon my head they plac'd a fruitless crown,
> And put a barren sceptre in my gripe,
> Thence to be wrench'd with a unlineal hand,
> No son of mine succeeding. If't be so,
> For Banquo's issue have I fil'd my mind;
> For them the gracious Duncan have I murder'd;
> Put rancours in the vessel of my peace
> Only for them; and mine eternal jewel
> Given to the common enemy of man,
> To make them kings, the seed of Banquo kings!

Presumably, Macbeth had entered upon his course from sheer personal ambition. Ironically, it is the more human part of Macbeth — his desire to have more than a limited personal satisfaction, his desire to found a line, his wish to pass something on to later generations — which prompts him to dispose of Banquo. There is, of course, a resentment against Banquo, but that resentment is itself closely related to Macbeth's desire to found a dynasty. Banquo, who has risked nothing, who has remained upright, who has not defiled himself, will have kings for children; Macbeth, none. Again, ironically, the Weird Sisters who have given Macbeth, so he has thought, the priceless gift of knowledge of the future, have given the real future to Banquo.

So Banquo's murder is decided upon, and accomplished. But Banquo's son escapes, and once more, the future has eluded Macbeth. The murder of Banquo thus becomes almost meaningless. This general point may be obvious enough, but we shall do well to note some of the further ways in which Shakespeare has pointed up the significance of Macbeth's war with the future.

When Macbeth, at the beginning of Scene vii, Act I, contemplates
Duncan's murder, it is the future over which he agonizes:

> If it were done, when 'tis done, then 'twere well
> It were done quickly; if the assassination
> Could trammel up the consequence, and catch
> With his surcease success; that but this blow
> Might be the be-all and the end-all here. ...

But the continuum of time cannot be partitioned off; the future is
implicit in the present. There is no net strong enough to trammel up
the consequence—not even in this world.

Lady Macbeth, of course, has fewer qualms. When Macbeth hesi-
tates to repudiate the duties which he owes Duncan—duties which, by
some accident of imagery perhaps—I hesitate to press the significance—he has earlier actually called "children"—Lady Macbeth cries
out that she is willing to crush her own child in order to gain the
crown:

> I have given suck, and know
> How tender 'tis to love the babe that milks me;
> I would, while it was smiling in my face,
> Have pluck'd my nipple from his boneless gums
> And dash'd the brains out, had I so sworn as you
> Have done to this.

Robert Penn Warren has made the penetrating observation that all
of Shakespeare's villains are rationalists. Lady Macbeth is certainly
of their company. She knows what she wants; and she is ruthless in
her consideration of means. She will always "catch the nearest way."
This is not to say that she ignores the problem of scruples, or that she
is ready to oversimplify psychological complexities. But scruples are
to be used to entangle one's enemies. One is not to become tangled
in the mesh of scruples himself. Even though she loves her husband
and though her ambition for herself is a part of her ambition for him,
still she seems willing to consider even Macbeth at times as pure
instrument, playing upon his hopes and fears and pride.

Her rationalism is quite sincere. She is apparently thoroughly
honest in declaring that

> The sleeping and the dead
> Are but as pictures; 'tis the eye of childhood
> That fears a painted devil. If he do bleed,
> I'll gild the faces of the grooms withal,
> For it must seem their guilt.

For her, there is no moral order: *guilt* is something like *gilt*—one can wash it off or paint it on. Her pun is not frivolous and it is deeply expressive.

Lady Macbeth abjures all pity; she is willing to unsex herself; and her continual taunt to Macbeth, when he falters, is that he is acting like a baby—not like a man. This "manhood" Macbeth tries to learn. He is a dogged pupil. For that reason he is almost pathetic when the shallow rationalism which his wife urges upon him fails. His tone is almost one of puzzled bewilderment at nature's unfairness in failing to play the game according to the rules—the rules which have applied to other murders:

> the time has been,
> That, when the brains were out, the man would die,
> And there an end; but now they rise again. ...

Yet, after the harrowing scene, Macbeth can say, with a sort of dogged weariness:

> Come, we'll to sleep. My strange and self-abuse
> Is the initiate fear that wants hard use:
> We are yet but young in deed.

Ironically, Macbeth is still echoing the dominant metaphor of Lady Macbeth's reproach. He has not yet attained to "manhood"; that *must* be the explanation. He has not yet succeeded in hardening himself into something inhuman.

Tempted by the Weird Sisters and urged on by his wife, Macbeth is thus caught between the irrational and the rational. There is a sense, of course, in which every man is caught between them. Man must try to predict and plan and control his destiny. That is man's fate; and the struggle, if he is to realize himself as a man, cannot be avoided. The question, of course, which has always interested the tragic dramatist involves the terms on which the struggle is accepted and the protagonist's attitude toward fate and toward himself. Macbeth in his general concern for the future is typical—is Every Man. He becomes the typical tragic protagonist when he yields to pride and *hybris*. The occasion for temptation is offered by the prophecy of the Weird Sisters. They offer him knowledge which cannot be arrived at rationally. They offer a key—if only a partial key—to what is otherwise unpredictable. Lady Macbeth, on the other hand, by employing a ruthless clarity of perception, by discounting all emotional claims, offers him the promise of bringing about the course of events which he desires.

Now, in the middle of the play, though he has not lost confidence and though, as he himself says, there can be no turning back, doubts have begun to arise; and he returns to the Weird Sisters to secure unambiguous answers to his fears. But, pathetically and ironically for Macbeth, in returning to the Weird Sisters, he is really trying to impose rationality on what sets itself forth plainly as irrational: that is, Macbeth would force a rigid control on a future which, by definition —by the very fact that the Weird Sisters already know it—stands beyond his manipulation.

It is because of his hopes for his own children and his fears of Banquo's that he has returned to the witches for counsel. It is altogether appropriate, therefore, that two of the apparitions by which their counsel is revealed should be babes, the crowned babe and the bloody babe.

For the babe signifies the future which Macbeth would control and cannot control. It is the unpredictable thing itself—as Yeats has put it magnificently, "The uncontrollable mystery on the bestial floor." It is the one thing that can justify, even in Macbeth's mind, the murders which he has committed. Earlier in the play, Macbeth had declared that if the deed could "trammel up the consequence," he would be willing to "jump the life to come." But he cannot jump the life to come. In his own terms he is betrayed. For it is idle to speak of jumping the life to come if one yearns to found a line of kings. It is the babe that betrays Macbeth—his own babes, most of all.

The logic of Macbeth's distraught mind, thus, forces him to make war on children, a war which in itself reflects his desperation and is a confession of weakness. Macbeth's ruffians, for example, break into Macduff's castle and kill his wife and children. The scene in which the innocent child prattles with his mother about his absent father, and then is murdered, is typical Shakespearean "fourth act" pathos. But the pathos is not adventitious; the scene ties into the inner symbolism of the play. For the child, in its helplessness, defies the murderers. Its defiance testifies to the force which threatens Macbeth and which Macbeth cannot destroy.

But we are not, of course, to placard the child as The Future in a rather stiff and mechanical allegory. *Macbeth* is no such allegory. Shakespeare's symbols are richer and more flexible than that. The babe signifies not only the future; it symbolizes all those enlarging purposes which make life meaningful, and it symbolizes, furthermore, all those emotional and—to Lady Macbeth—irrational ties which make man more than a machine—which render him human. It signifies pre-eminently the pity which Macbeth, under Lady Macbeth's tutelage, would wean himself of as something "unmanly." Lady Macbeth's great speeches early in the play become brilliantly ironical when we realize that Shakespeare is using the same symbol for the unpredictable future that he uses for human compassion. Lady Macbeth is willing to go to any length to grasp the future: she would willingly dash out the brains of her own child if it stood in her way to that future. But this is to repudiate the future, for the child is its symbol.

Shakespeare does not, of course, limit himself to the symbolism of the child: he makes use of other symbols of growth and development, notably that of the plant. And this plant symbolism patterns itself to reflect the development of the play. For example, Banquo says to the Weird Sisters, early in the play:

> If you can look into the seeds of time,
> And say which grain will grow and which will not,
> Speak then to me. ...

A little later, on welcoming Macbeth, Duncan says to him:

> I have begun to plant thee, and will labour
> To make thee full of growing.

After the murder of Duncan, Macbeth falls into the same metaphor when he comes to resolve on Banquo's death. The Weird Sisters, he reflects, had hailed Banquo as

> father to a line of kings.
> Upon my head they placed a fruitless crown,
> And put a barren sceptre in my gripe. ...

Late in the play, Macbeth sees himself as the winter-stricken tree:

> I have liv'd long enough: my way of life
> Is fall'n into the sear, the yellow leaf. ...

The plant symbolism, then, supplements the child symbolism. At points it merges with it, as when Macbeth ponders bitterly that he has damned himself.

> To make them kings, the seed of Banquo kings!

And, in at least one brilliant example, the plant symbolism unites with the clothes symbolism. It is a crowning irony that one of the Weird Sisters' prophecies on which Macbeth has staked his hopes is fulfilled when Birnam Wood comes to Dunsinane. For, in a sense,

Macbeth is here hoist on his own petard. Macbeth, who has invoked night to "Scarf up the tender eye of pitiful day," and who has, again and again, used the "false face" to "hide what the false heart doth know," here has the trick turned against him. But the garment which cloaks the avengers is the living green of nature itself, and nature seems, to the startled eyes of his sentinels, to be rising up against him.

But it is the babe, the child, that dominates the symbolism. Most fittingly, the last of the prophecies in which Macbeth has placed his confidence, concerns the child: and Macbeth comes to know the final worst when Macduff declares to him that he was not "born of woman" but was from his "mother's womb/ Untimely ripp'd." The babe here has defied even the thing which one feels may reasonably be predicted of him—his time of birth. With Macduff's pronouncement, the unpredictable has broken through the last shred of the net of calculation. The future cannot be trammelled up. The naked babe confronts Macbeth to pronounce his doom.

The passage with which we began this essay, then, is an integral part of a larger context, and of a very rich context:

> And pity, like a naked new-born babe,
> Striding the blast, or heaven's cherubim, hors'd
> Upon the sightless couriers of the air,
> Shall blow the horrid deed in every eye,
> That tears shall drown the wind.

Pity is like the naked babe, the most sensitive and helpless thing; yet, almost as soon as the comparison is announced, the symbol of weakness begins to turn into a symbol of strength; for the babe, though newborn, is pictured as "Striding the blast" like an elemental force— like "heaven's cherubim, hors'd/ Upon the sightless couriers of the air." We can give an answer to the question put earlier: is Pity like the human and helpless babe, or powerful as the angel that rides the winds? It is both; and it is strong because of its very weakness. The paradox is inherent in the situation itself; and it is the paradox that will destroy the overbrittle rationalism on which Macbeth founds his career.

For what will it avail Macbeth to cover the deed with the blanket of the dark if the elemental forces that ride the winds will blow the horrid deed in every eye? And what will it avail Macbeth to clothe himself in "manliness"—to become bloody, bold, and resolute,—if he is to find himself again and again, viewing his bloody work through the "eye of childhood/ That fears a painted devil"? Certainly, the final and climactic appearance of the babe symbol merges all the contradictory elements of the symbol. For, with Macduff's statement about his birth, the naked babe rises before Macbeth as not only the future that eludes calculation but as avenging angel as well.

The clothed daggers and the naked babe—mechanism and life—instrument and end—death and birth—that which should be left bare and clean and that which should be clothed and warmed—these are facets of two of the great symbols which run throughout the play. They are not the only symbols, to be sure; they are not the most obvious symbols: darkness and blood appear more often. But with a flexibility which must amaze the reader, the image of the garment and the image of the babe are so used as to encompass an astonishingly large area of the total situation. And between them—the naked babe, essential humanity, humanity stripped down to the naked thing itself, and yet as various as the future—and the various garbs which humanity assumes, the robes of honor, the hypocrite's disguise, the inhuman "manliness" with which Macbeth endeavors to cover up his essential humanity—between them, they furnish Shakespeare with his most subtle and ironically telling instruments.

Shakespeare and the "New" Critics

by Oscar James Campbell

One of the sanest of recent applications of the new critical method to a Shakespearian play is an essay on *Macbeth*, entitled "The Naked Babe and the Cloak of Manliness,"[1] The article illustrates the virtues of the method but also exemplifies its dangers, even though it be applied by a critic of unusual sensitivity and insight. Mr. Brooks, discovering two principal chains of imagery in *Macbeth*, one composed of garments or "old clothes," the other of babes, undertakes to prove that each chain subserves a deep imaginative unity. Since he realizes that what is at stake in his investigation is the whole matter of the relation of Shakespeare's imagery to the structure of the play, he proceeds with caution and (if his premises be granted) with adequate logic.

Miss Spurgeon, in her study of the images in *Macbeth*, pointed out that "the idea constantly recurs that Macbeth's new honors sit ill upon him, like a loose and badly fitting garment belonging to someone else."[2] And she illustrates the point by showing how many times Shakespeare repeats and varies the clothes image in order to keep before our minds "this imaginative picture of a small ignoble man encumbered and degraded by garments unsuited to him." The poet's manipulation of this image, as described by Miss Spurgeon, is the reverse of metaphysical; it is direct and simple. The imaginative significance of Banquo's remark as he observes Macbeth ruminating over the "supernatural soliciting" of the witches—

> New honours come upon him,
> Like our strange garments, cleave not to their mould
> But with the aid of use   (I. iii. 144-146)—

"Shakespeare and the 'New' Critics," by Oscar James Campbell. From James G. McManaway, Giles E. Dawson, and Edwin E. Willoughby, eds., *Joseph Quincy Adams Memorial Studies* (Charlottesville, Va.: The University Press of Virginia, 1948), Section II, pp. 85-91. Copyright © 1948 by The University Press of Virginia. Reprinted by permission of the publisher.

[1]This essay appears in Cleanth Brooks' *The Well Wrought Urn* (1947), pp. 21-46. See pp. 34-53 in this volume.

[2]*"Shakespeare's Imagery"* [see this volume p. 13].

is easily grasped without the intervention of a new critic. So is Angus's comment upon Macbeth's conduct after his accession to power:

> Now does he feel his title
> Hang loose about him, like a giant's robe
> Upon a dwarfish thief.   (V. ii. 20-22)

These two passages are typical of Shakespeare's use of the clothes metaphor as a descriptive tag to pin upon Macbeth.

Mr Brooks, however, finds such simple employment of the figure merely an adumbration of its more subtle manifestations. After glancing with approval at Miss Spurgeon's analysis, he asserts that these undisguised appearances of the metaphor are paralleled by a series of cloaking or masking images, variants of garment figures. The purpose of those figures is to suggest that throughout the play Macbeth is seeking to hide his "disgraceful self" from his own eyes as well as from the eyes of others. Mr. Brooks seeks to prove that the cloaking images form a chain, in the manner of the metaphysicals new and old, to keep alive the ironical contrast between the wretched creature that Macbeth really is and the pompous disguises he assumes to conceal the fact.

In attempting to build a structure out of the clothes images Mr. Brooks is forced to distort the meaning of more than one passage. This is evident in the variant interpretation he offers for Lady Macbeth's

> Come, thick night,
> And pall thee in the dunnest smoke of hell,
> That my keen knife sees not the wound it makes,
> Nor heaven peep through the blanket of the dark
> To cry, Hold, Hold!   (I. v. 50-54)

Mr. Brooks admits that it is natural to think of the "keen knife" as in Lady Macbeth's hand and that she is begging the night to be so dark that even her knife, much less herself, may not see the wound it makes. The interpretation is more than natural, considering the fact that the image comes at the end of a speech in which she seeks to suppress her woman's nature so that she can be capable of the horrid deed.

But since the figure thus interpreted cannot serve as a link in the chain the critic is forging, Mr. Brooks offers the over-ingenious suggestion that the "keen knife" may be Macbeth himself. Thus interpreted, the figure can be forced to serve as one more indication of the efforts of the two murderers to hide from themselves what they are and what they do. Lady Macbeth would then be invoking the pall, the clothing of death, to blanket the horrid deed from the reluctant doer. But such an interpretation seems to this writer to be strained beyond the limits of credulity.

It is obvious that *Macbeth* contains much clothes imagery, but it is equally undeniable that Shakespeare used it in his own characteristic fashion. Once having employed the figure as a swift and startling method of characterizing his villain hero, the poet found the image and the word so securely lodged in his mind that it arose repeatedly while he was at work on his drama. And instead of discarding it every time it demanded expression, he subtly varied its form and employed it on many occasions to intensify crucial moments in the action. A striking example of putting the figure to an original use occurs when, at the end of a highly mannered passage, Macbeth describes the murderers' daggers as "unmannerly breeched with gore." Mr. Brooks properly characterizes this image as vivid and fantastic. But his efforts to make it play a part in developing the disguise motif seems as fantastic as the metaphor. The daggers, naked except for their red breeches, are not only "unmannerly" but have also been clothed, or so he believes, in a horrible masquerade in order to play in this disguise a villainous role. For their natural guise was honorable nakedness, the form in which they could have guarded the King. This interpretation quite ignores the value of the metaphor for the speech in which it occurs. There it flashes a sudden light upon Macbeth's state of mind at the moment when he utters it. Shakespeare has designed the series of extravagant images—of which the daggers "unmannerly breeched with gore" is the last—as a means of revealing Macbeth's neurotic embarrassment, which is here on the verge of betraying his guilt to Macduff, Malcolm, and Donalbain. In other words, the figure epitomizes the murderers' state of mind and nerves at one of the play's high emotional moments. Mr. Brooks' analysis of the various clothes images does not establish the facts he desires. But it has the unconscious merit of throwing into sharp relief the difference between Shakespeare's habitual use of figurative language and the methods of the metaphysical poets, which the new critics falsely assume Shakespeare to have adopted.

Mr. Brooks' analysis of Shakespeare's employment of the image of the babe is less free of bias than his treatment of the clothes figure and leads to a less valid conclusion. He begins with a brilliant interpretation of some lines which many commentators have stigmatized as pure fustian:

> And pity, like a naked new-born babe,
> Striding the blast, or heaven's cherubim, hors'd

> Upon the sightless couriers of the air,
> Shall blow the horrid deed in every eye,
> That tears shall drown the wind.   (I. vii. 21)

The poet means, so says Mr. Brooks, that the nature of pity is para-doxical. When first aroused it seems to be as helpless as a new born babe. Yet when it is blown into the hearts and minds of multitudes of men, it becomes stronger than the blasts of tempestuous wind. That is, its strength lies in its very weakness.

Mr. Brooks' close attention to this passage has led him to note many other references to babes in *Macbeth*. "Sometimes," he writes, "it is a character such as Macduff's child" (who is not a babe at all); "some-times a symbol, like the crowned babe and the bloody babe which are raised by the witches;...sometimes in a metaphor." This babe, the critic arbitrarily decides, "signifies the future which Macbeth would control and cannot control." Mr. Brooks makes this identification in spite of the fact that in the passage he has just analyzed the babe is a symbol of something quite different. But not satisfied with this con-crete use of the symbol Mr. Brooks explains that "the babe signifies not only the future; it symbolizes all those enlarging purposes which make life meaningful, and it symbolizes, furthermore, all those emo-tional and—to Lady Macbeth—irrational ties which make man more than a machine—which render him human." By this time the hard concrete core of the symbol has developed so amorphous an aura that its "burning center" has been almost completely obscured. By inter-preting the babe as a recurrent symbol of the future Mr. Brooks is able to discover that Macbeth's tragedy is that of man making futile efforts to control the future. But this erratic, neo-Hegelian judgment reduces the rich complexity of Macbeth's human nature to a bare general proposition. His tragedy lies not in a failure of his efforts to impose his will upon the future but in the multitudinous fears and super-stitions that form the psychological punishment for his crime. What-ever the value of imagery as an objective correlative of emotion, it obviously must not be interpreted in such a way as to contradict directly the clear meaning of the plot.

If Mr. Brooks' conclusions be false, it is important to discover at what points his method has been at fault. In general his errors of judgment result from efforts to force all the references to babes into one connected system of imagery to form a structural principal for the drama. For example, Macbeth's famous soliloquy ending

> If th' assassination
> Could trammel up the consequence, and catch
> With his surcease, success; that but this blow

> Might be the be-all and the end-all here,
> But here, upon this bank and shoal of time,
> We'd jump the life to come   (I. vii. 2-7)

to Mr. Brooks means that Macbeth is agonizing over the future. But Macbeth's case is hopeless, he proceeds, because "the continuum of time cannot be partitioned off, the future is implicit in the present." Such recourse to a philosophical generality is perverse. Macbeth, like all murderers in Elizabethan plays, is afraid, not of his inability to control the future, but of the knife in the hands of a human avenger. This fear he expresses in the lines:

> We but teach
> Bloody instructions, which, being taught, return
> To plague the inventor.   (I. vii. 8-10)

This expectation of inevitable revenge is the reason why his fears in Banquo stick deep—why, in spite of the witches' assurance that he need fear no man of woman born, he fears Macduff so greatly that he orders his death.

One reason for Mr. Brooks' misunderstanding of the above passage is his misinterpretation of the phrase "the life to come." In its context it clearly refers to life after death and not, as Mr. Brooks thinks, to the future of Macbeth and his line in this world. Can it be that the critic has taken "jump" to mean "leap over"—that is, "skip"—instead of the correct "risk"? His following statement suggests this as a distinct possibility. "It is idle," he says, "to speak of jumping the life to come if one yearns to found a line of kings."

Mr. Brooks forces other passages into distorted shapes in his valiant effort to forge a chain of imagery out of materials extracted from the poetry. For example, he gives a sophistical interpretation of one of Lady Macbeth's most revealing exclamations. Her scornful cry that she would rather have torn her baby from her breast and dashed out its brains than be so cowardly as to fail to kill Duncan, as her husband had sworn to do. This, says the critic, means that she is willing to go to any lengths to grasp the future. But her cry, Mr. Brooks continues, is extremely ironical because "she will grasp the future by repudiating the future of which the child is the symbol." This over-ingenious reading obscures and enfeebles the stark simplicity of Lady Macbeth's utterance. What she says to her husband is this: Rather than be such an irresolute coward as you now are, I had rather be guilty of the most fiendishly unnatural deed of which a mother is capable.

More than once Brooks forces upon an image an interpretation which murder to him. They do not foretell that Macbeth will murder Duncan in order to be king. They foretell that Banquo will not be king but that he will be greater than Macbeth because he will father a line of kings, and they let that prophecy, too, suggest murder to Macbeth. They do not foretell that Macbeth will murder Banquo. With the help of evil powers whom they call their "masters" they let Macbeth know through visions that he is to beware Macduff, that he shall be harmed by none of woman born, that he shall never be vanquished until Birnam Wood shall come to Dunsinane Hill, and that Banquo's issue shall indeed bring forth a line of kings; and they let these visions give Macbeth both fear and rash confidence and stir him again to undertake murder. They do not foretell, and neither do their masters, that he will murder Macduff's wife, children, and servants.

by the wildest stretch of the imagination, it cannot be made to bear. For example, he insists that when Macduff's little boy defies the murderers the child, whom he persists in calling a babe, testifies to the strength of the future, the force that threatens Macbeth and which he cannot destroy. The child, whose real dramatic function, besides the evocation of pity, is to show the wild killer that Macbeth has become in his efforts to kill fear itself, in Mr. Brooks' view "ties into the inner symbolism of the play." The truth is that Shakespeare has not used the image of the babe any more in the manner of a metaphysical poet than he did that of the clothes image. The word and the image reappeared in the poet's mind, but each time he used it for an immediate imaginative purpose relevant only to a specific situation.

Macbeth and the Kingdom of Heaven

by Roy Walker

The kingdom in *Macbeth* shadows forth the kingdom of heaven on earth, obscured for a time by the blanket of the dark but never sundered from heaven. The tragedy is focused on the destruction of awareness of the kingdom of heaven within and the attempt of the human vassals of evil to usurp the divine-temporal kingship. But Malcolm and Donalbain, Fleance and Macduff, the pious English King and Siward, the rebellious thanes and the anonymous Old Man, the slain Banquo and Macduff's little son, are all conscious in some degree of being the children of Saint Columba, citizens of a kingdom of which the great bond they dimly read is carried in their own souls. Hamlet is noble despite his world; the world is noble despite Macbeth. If the central tragic figures reflect the spiritual experiences of the poet, we may say that the desperate misanthropy of *Hamlet* has become the agonised *mea culpa* of *Macbeth*. The tempest-tossed ship has rounded the sterile promontory, and as the storm of evil abates a little the shores of Prospero's magic island are already distantly visible to the pilot's prophetic eye.

The Witches

by Willard Farnham

It will be worth our while to begin an examination of the world of *Macbeth* by looking closely at the three witches and the part given them to play. Before we make up our minds about the guilt of the hero and, finally, the meaning of the tragedy, we must first decide what power these beings wield over the actions and fortunes of the hero. They are witches having the forms of repulsive old women, but they are not mortal witches such as the law might get its hands upon and put to death in the England or Scotland of Shakespeare's day. They are "weird sisters," but the word "weird" as applied to them cannot mean that they have control over Macbeth's destiny and compel him to do all that he does. Macbeth is certainly no mere puppet moving under their manipulation. Nothing is clearer than that Shakespeare writes of Macbeth as of a man who has free will so far, at least, as the choice of good or evil is concerned, and who in choosing evil creates for himself physical misfortune and a spiritual hell on earth. In what they do the witches show themselves to have a power over Macbeth that is limited, however strong it may be. They are supernatural agents of evil, and in working to make fair into foul they reveal both the capacities and the incapacities that the Christian tradition has attributed to devils. They tempt Macbeth to do evil, and tempt him with great subtlety. They cannot force him to do it.

The witches reveal a fate for Macbeth and imply that a part of what will come to him must come, but they reveal no fate of evil-doing for him and never, even by suggestion, bind him to evil-doing. As prophets they are "imperfect speakers." By their imperfect speaking they tempt him to commit crimes for which he is to assume full moral responsibility, a responsibility so complete that it will be not only for doing but also for forming the thought of doing, each criminal deed. They foretell that Macbeth will be king, and they let that prophecy sugge

Manhood and Valor in Macbeth

by Eugene M. Waith

In *Macbeth*, more clearly than in *Hamlet*, there is an explicit contrast between two ideals of manhood. Macbeth is a soldier whose valor we hear praised throughout the play. To the "bleeding Sergeant" he is "brave Macbeth," to Duncan "valiant cousin, worthy gentleman"; Ross calls him "Bellona's bridegroom." To be courageous is to be "manly," as the soldier understands that word, and hence at the end of the play, when Macduff reveals the fatal circumstances of his birth, Macbeth says that the news has "cow'd my better part of man," to which Macduff replies, "Then yield thee, coward" (V. viii. 18, 23). After the death of the hero physical valor is given final emphasis in a speech of Ross to Siward:

> Your son, my lord, has paid a soldier's debt.
> He only liv'd but till he was a man,
> The which no sooner had his prowess confirm'd
> In the unshrinking station where he fought
> But like a man he died.   (V. viii. 39-43)

In all these comments there is implied one ideal—the soldier's, or as Plutarch says, the Roman's ideal—of what it is to be a man. Lady Macbeth clearly subscribes to it when she urges her husband to "screw his courage to the sticking place." In her speeches she makes explicit the contrast between the sexes which underlies this concept of manhood. To strengthen her resolve she appeals to the spirits to "unsex me here":

> Come to my woman's breasts
> And take my milk for gall....   (I. v. 48-49)

She fears that Macbeth has too much of the "milk of human kindness," and he himself says to her,

"Manhood and Valor in *Macbeth.*"ⁱFrom Eugene M. Waith, *Manhood and Valor in Two Shakespearean Tragedies*, ELH: A Journal of English Literary History, vol. 17, no. 4 (1950), pp. 265-68. Copyright © 1950 by Johns Hopkins University Press. Reprinted by permission.

> Bring forth men-children only;
> For thy undaunted mettle should compose
> Nothing but males.   (I. vii. 72-74)

Thus not to be a man is to be effeminate.

In this same scene, however, Macbeth introduces another antithesis
—that of man and beast. When Lady Macbeth taunts him for his
cowardice, he replies,

> I dare do all that may become a man;
> Who dares do more is none.   (I. vii. 46-47)

That Lady Macbeth understands his implication is clear from her
scoffing question:

> What beast was't then
> That made you break this enterprise to me?   (I. vii. 47-48)

The important point is that Macbeth's distinction rests, as we can see
from his soliloquy at the opening of the scene, upon his awareness of
the moral nature of man. His mental torment grows out of the conflict
between the narrow concept of man as the courageous male and the
more inclusive concept of man as a being whose moral nature distinguishes him from the beasts. The first is that debased ideal of manhood censured by Milles, while the second is the "reall excellencie of
humaine Nature" based on "another kinde of strength and courage,
then that which is proper to brute Beasts onely"

Shakespeare keeps the two concepts before us throughout the play.
The pangs of Macbeth's conscience after the murder (note his inability
to say "amen") are no more than effeminate or childish fears to Lady
Macbeth (II. ii). In urging his hired assassins to the murder of Banquo,
Macbeth echos his wife, contrasting patience and piety with the manhood necessary to perform the bloody deed (III. i). When Banquo's
ghost brings on Macbeth's "fit," Lady Macbeth asks him, "Are you a
man?" And then:

> O, these flaws and starts
> (Impostors to true fear) would well become
> A woman's story at a winter's fire....
> What, quite unmann'd in folly?
>
> (III. iv. 63-65, 73)

Macbeth says "What man dare, I dare" (III. iv. 99).

In the puzzling scene (IV. iii) in which Malcolm tests Macduff,

Macbeth's formidable antagonist is established as the exact antithesis of the sort of man Lady Macbeth admires. When Malcolm accuses himself of all Macbeth's sins, Macduff demonstrates his "truth and honor" by his horrified rejection of Malcolm, and thus reveals the moral qualifications of "true" manhood. Then, when Ross tells him of the murders of Lady Macduff and of his children, Macduff appears so overwhelmed by grief that Malcolm says to him, "Dispute it like a man."[1] His reply is most significant:

> I shall do so;
> But I must also feel it as a man.
> I cannot but remember such things were
> That were most precious to me. Did heaven look on
> And would not take their part? Sinful Macduff,
> They were all struck for thee! Naught that I am,
> Not for their own demerits, but for mine,
> Fell slaughter on their souls.   (IV. iii. 220-27)

Macduff is a complete man: he is a valiant soldier, ready to perform "manly" deeds, but is neither ashamed of "humane" feelings nor unaware of his moral responsibilities. This combination is emphasized in his next speech, where he shows clearly that his admirable sensibility does not make him womanish:

> O, I could play the woman with mine eyes
> And braggart with my tongue! But, gentle heavens,
> Cut short all intermission. Front to front
> Bring thou this fiend of Scotland and myself.
> Within my sword's length set him. If he scape,
> Heaven forgive him too!   (IV. iii. 230-35)

Malcolm's comment is: "This tune goes manly."

The development of Macbeth's character is a triumph for Lady Macbeth's ideal, for conscience is stifled, and Macbeth, like Hamlet, becomes increasingly "bloody, bold and resolute." His deliberate decision, against the dictates of his better judgment, to be a "man" in this narrow sense of the word is one of the most important manifestations of the evil which dominates the entire play: to his subjects Macbeth now seems a devil. Shakespeare's insistence upon this narrow-

---

[1]Malcom's speech is sometimes interpreted to mean "Contend with your sorrow," but since he has just urged Macduff to express his sorrow (II. 209-10), it seems more likely that he means "Avenge yourself like a man." In both interpretations manliness is equated with courage.

ing of character is also a commentary on Macbeth's ambition. In "the swelling act of the imperial theme," the hero becomes fatally diminished. The final stage of the development is revealed in Macbeth's speeches at the time of Lady Macbeth's death. Here we are confronted by the supreme irony that when she dies, tortured by the conscience she despised, Macbeth is so perfectly hardened, so completely the soldier that she wanted him to be, that he is neither frightened by the "night-shriek" nor greatly moved by the news of her death. Death has no meaning for him, and life is

> a tale
> Told by an idiot, full of sound and fury,
> Signifying nothing.   (V. v. 26-28)

Though Macduff's announcement that he was "untimely ripp'd" from his mother's womb causes Macbeth to falter, he dies a courageous soldier, and hence, according to that narrower definition, "like a man." It is appropriate that his death is immediately followed by the last statement of the soldierly standard of values in the tribute Ross pays to Siward's son: "Like a man he died." But on the battlefield is Macduff, who is even more of a man—a soldier who fights only in a good cause, and in whose nature valor is not the sole virtue.

Macbeth as the Imitation of an Action

by Francis Fergusson

I propose to attempt to illustrate the view that *Macbeth* may be understood as "the imitation of an action," in approximately Aristotle's sense of this phrase.

The word "action"—*praxis*—as Aristotle uses it in the *Poetics,* does not mean outward deeds or events, but something much more like "purpose" or "aim." Perhaps our word "motive" suggests most of its meaning. Dante (who in this respect is a sophisticated Aristotelian) uses the phrase *moto spiral,* spiritual movement, to indicate *praxis.* In Aristotle's own writings *praxis* is usually rational, a movement of the will in the light of the mind. But Dante's *moto spiral* refers to all modes of the spirit's life, all of its directions, or focuses, or motives, including those of childhood, dream, drunkenness, or passion, which are hardly rationalized at all. When using Aristotle's definition for the analysis of modern drama it is necessary to generalize his notion of action in this way, to include movements of the spirit in response to sensuous or emotionally charged images, as well as consciously willed purpose. But this seems to me a legitimate extension of the basic concept; and I do not think it does real violence to Aristotle's meaning....

I remarked that action is not outward deeds or events; but on the other hand, there can be no action without resulting deeds. We guess at a man's action by way of what he does, his outward and visible deeds. We are aware that our own action, or motive, produces deeds of some sort as soon as it exists. Now the plot of a play is the arrangement of outward deeds or incidents, and the dramatist uses it, as Aristotle tells us, as the first means of imitating the action. He arranges a set of incidents which point to the action or motive from which they spring. You may say that the action is the spiritual content of the tragedy— the playwright's inspiration—and the plot defines its existence as an

"*Macbeth* as the Imitation of an Action" by Francis Fergusson, from *English Institute Essays 1951* (New York: Columbia University Press, 1952), pp. 31-43, and reprinted in W. K. Wimsatt, Jr., ed., *Explication as Criticism: Selected Papers from the English Institute* (1963), pp. 85-87 and 88-89. Reprinted by permission of the publisher.

intelligible *play*. Thus, you cannot have a play without both plot and action; yet the distinction between plot and action is as fundamental as that between form and matter. The action is the matter; the plot is the "first form," or, as Aristotle puts it, the "soul," of the tragedy....

The action of the play as a whole is best expressed in a phrase which Macbeth himself uses in Act II, scene 3, the aftermath of the murder. Macbeth is trying to appear innocent, but everything he says betrays his clear sense of his own evil motivation, or action. Trying to excuse his murder of Duncan's grooms, he says,

> The expedition of my violent love [for Duncan, he means]
> Outran the pauser, reason.

It is the phrase "to outrun the pauser, reason," which seems to me to describe the action, or motive, of the play as a whole. Macbeth, of course, literally means that his love for Duncan was so strong and swift that it got ahead of his reason, which would have counseled a pause. But in the same way we have seen his greed and ambition outrun his reason when he committed the murder; and in the same way all of the characters, in the irrational darkness of Scotland's evil hour, are compelled in their action to strive beyond what they can see by reason alone. Even Malcolm and Macduff, as we shall see, are compelled to go beyond reason in the action which destroys Macbeth and ends the play.

But let me consider the phrase itself for a moment. To "outrun" reason suggests an impossible stunt, like lifting oneself by one's own bootstraps. It also suggests a competition or race, like those of nightmare, which cannot be won. As for the word "reason," Shakespeare associates it with nature and nature's order, in the individual soul, in society, and in the cosmos. To outrun reason is thus to violate nature itself, to lose the bearings of common sense and of custom, and to move into a spiritual realm bounded by the irrational darkness of Hell one way, and the superrational grace of faith the other way. As the play develops before us, all the modes of this absurd, or evil, or supernatural, action are attempted, the last being Malcolm's and Macduff's acts of faith....

"Outrunning reason" looks purely evil in the beginning, and at the end we see how it may be good, an act of faith beyond reason.

The Structure of *Macbeth*

by R. S. Crane

Before we can understand a poem as an artistic structure we must understand it as a grammatical structure made up of successive words, sentences, paragraphs, and speeches which give us both meanings in the ordinary sense of that term and signs from which we may infer what the speakers, whether characters or narrators, are like and what they are thinking, feeling, or doing. The great temptation for critics who are not trained and practicing scholars is to take this understanding for granted or to think that it may easily be obtained at second hand by consulting the works of scholars. This is an illusion, just as it is an illusion in scholars to suppose that they can see, without training in criticism, all the problems which their distinctive methods are fitted to solve. The ideal would be that all critics should be scholars and all scholars critics; but, although there ought to be the closest correlation of the two functions in practice, they are nevertheless distinct in nature and in the kinds of hypotheses to which they lead. The hypotheses of interpretation are concerned with the meanings and implications in texts that result from their writers' expressive intentions in setting down particular words and constructions and arranging these in particular sequences. Such meanings and implications, indeed, are forms, of which words and sentences are the matter; but they are forms of a kind that can appear in any sort of discourse, however unpoetic. They are to be interpreted by resolving the forms into the elements which poems share with the common speech or writing and the common thought and experience of the times when they were written; and this requires the use of techniques and principles quite different from any that poetic theory can afford: the techniques and principles of historical grammar, of the analysis and history of ideas, of the history of literary conventions, manners, and so on, and

"The Structure of Macbeth" (editor's title). From R. S. Crane, *The Languages of Criticism and the Structure of Poetry* (Toronto: University of Toronto Press, 1953), pp. 168-73. Copyright © Canada, 1953, by University of Toronto Press. Reprinted by permission of the publisher.

the still more general techniques and principles, seldom methodized, by which we construe characters and actions in everyday life.

The hypotheses of criticism, on the contrary, are concerned with the shaping principles, peculiar to the poetic arts, which account in any work for the power of its grammatical materials, in the particular ordering given to these, to move our opinions and feelings in such-and-such a way. They will be of two sorts according as the questions to which they are answers relate to the principles by which poetic works have been constructed as wholes of certain definite kinds or to the reasons which connect a particular part of a given work, directly or indirectly, with such a principle by way of the poetic problems it sets for the writer at this point. And there can be no good practical criticism in this mode in which both sorts are not present; for although the primary business of the critic is with the particulars of any work he studies down to its minuter details of diction and rhythm, he can never exhibit the artistic problems involved in these or find other than extrapoetic reasons for their solutions without the guidance of an explitit definition of the formal whole which they have made possible.

A single work will suffice to illustrate both kinds of critical hypotheses as well as the relation between them, and I will begin by considering what idea of the governing form of *Macbeth* appears to accord best with the facts of that play and the sequence of emotions it arouses in us. I need not say again why it seems to me futile to look for an adequate structural formula for *Macbeth* in any of the more "imaginative" directions commonly taken by recent criticism; I shall assume, therefore, without argument, that we have to do, not with a lyric "statement of evil" or an allegory of the workings of sin in the soul and the state or a metaphysical myth of destruction followed by recreation or a morality play with individualized characters rather than types, but simply with an imitative tragic drama based on historical materials. To call it an imitative tragic drama, however, does not carry us very far; it merely limits roughly the range of possible forms we have to consider. Among these are the contrasting plot-forms embodied respectively in *Othello* and in *Richard III:* the first a tragic plot-form in the classic sense of Aristotle's analysis in *Poetics* 13; the second a plot-form which Aristotle rejected as nontragic but which appealed strongly to tragic poets in the Renaissance—a form of serious action designed to arouse moral indignation for the deliberately unjust and seemingly prospering acts of the protagonist and moral satisfaction at his subsequent ruin. The plot-form of *Macbeth* clearly involves elements which assimilate it now to the one and now to the other of both these kinds. The action of the play is twofold, and one of its aspects is the punitive action of Malcolm, Macduff, and their friends which in the end brings about the protagonist's downfall and death. The characters here are all good men, whom Macbeth has unforgivably wronged, and their cause is the unqualifiedly just cause of freeing Scotland from a bloody tyrant and restoring the rightful line of kings. All this is made clear in the representation not only directly through the speeches and acts of the avengers but indirectly by those wonderfully vivid devices of imagery and general thought in which modern critics have found the central value and meaning of the play as a whole; and our responses, when this part of the action is before us, are such as are clearly dictated by the immediate events and the poetic commentary: we desire, that is, the complete success of the counteraction and this as speedily as possible before Macbeth can commit further horrors. We desire this, however—and that is what at once takes the plot-form out of the merely retributive class—not only for the sake of humanity and Scotland but also for the sake of Macbeth himself. For what most sharply distinguishes our view of Macbeth from that of his victims and enemies is that, whereas they see him from the outside only, we see him also, throughout the other action of the play—the major action—from the inside, as he sees himself; and what we see thus is a moral spectacle the emotional quality of which, for the impartial observer, is not too far removed from the tragic *dynamis* specified in the *Poetics*. This is not to say that the main action of *Macbeth* is not significantly different, in several respects, from the kind of tragic action which Aristotle envisages. The change is not merely from good to bad fortune, but from a good state of character to a state in which the hero is almost, but not quite, transformed into a monster; and the tragic act which initiates the change, and still more the subsequent unjust acts which this entails, are acts done—unlike Othello's killing of Desdemona—in full knowledge of their moral character. We cannot, therefore, state the form of this action in strictly Aristotelian terms, but the form is none the less one that involves, like tragedy in Aristotle's sense, the arousal and catharsis of painful emotions for, and not merely with respect to, the protagonist—emotions for which the terms pity and fear are not entirely inapplicable.

Any adequate hypothesis about the structure of *Macbeth*, then, would have to take both of these sets of facts into account. For both of the views we are given of the hero are true: he is in fact, in terms of the nature and objective consequences of his deeds, what Macduff and Malcolm say he is throughout Acts IV and V, but he is also—and the form of the play is really the interaction of the two views in our opinions and emotions—what we ourselves see him to be as we witness the workings of his mind before the murder of Duncan, then after the murder, and finally when, at the end, all his illusions and hopes gone, he faces Macduff. He is one who commits monstrous deeds without becoming wholly a monster, since his knowledge of the right principle is never altogether obscured, though it is almost so in Act IV. We can understand such a person and hence feel fear and pity of a kind for him because he is only doing upon a grander scale and with deeper guilt and more terrifying consequences for himself and others what we can, without too much difficulty, imagine ourselves doing, however less extremely, in circumstances generally similar. For the essential story of *Macbeth* is that of a man, not naturally depraved, who has fallen under the compulsive power of an imagined better state for himself which he can attain only by acting contrary to his normal habits and feelings; who attains this state and then finds that he must continue to act thus, and even worse, in order to hold on to what he has got; who persists and becomes progressively hardened morally in the process; and who then, ultimately, when the once alluring good is about to be taken away from him, faces the loss in terms of what is left of his original character. It is something like this moral universal that underlies, I think, and gives emotional form to the main action of *Macbeth.* It is a form that turns upon the difference between what seemingly advantageous crime appears to be in advance to a basically good but incontinent man and what its moral consequences for such a man inevitably are; and the catharsis is effected not merely by the man's deserved overthrow but by his own inner suffering and by his discovery, before it is too late, of what he had not known before he began to act. If we are normal human human beings we must abhor his crimes; yet we cannot completely abhor but must rather pity the man himself, and even when he seems most the monster (as Macbeth does in Act IV) we must still wish for such an outcome as will be best, under the circumstances, not merely for Scotland but for him.

But if this, or something close to it, is indeed the complex emotional structure intended in *Macbeth,* then we have a basis for defining with some precision the various problems of incident, character, thought, imagery, diction, and representation which confronted Shakespeare in writing the play, and hence a starting-point for discussing, in detail, the rationale of its parts. Consider—to take only one instance—the final scene. In the light of the obvious consequences of the form I have attributed to the play as a whole, it is not difficult to state what the main problems at this point are. If the catharsis of the tragedy is to be complete, we must be made to feel both that Macbeth is being killed in a just cause and that his state of mind and the circumstances of his death are such as befit a man who, for all his crimes, has not altogether lost our pity and good will. We are of course prepared for this double response by all that has gone before, and, most immediately, in the earlier scenes of Act V, by the fresh glimpses we are given of the motivation of the avengers and by Macbeth's soliloquies. But it will clearly be better if the dual effect can be sustained until the very end; and this requires, on the one hand, that we should be vividly reminded once more of Macbeth's crimes and the justified hatred they have caused and of the prospect of a new and better time which his death holds out for Scotland, and, on the other hand, that we should be allowed to take satisfaction, at last, in the manner in which Macbeth himself behaves. The artistic triumph of the scene lies in the completeness with which both problems are solved: the first in the words and actions of Macduff, the speeches about young Siward, and Malcolm's closing address; the second by a variety of devices, both of invention and of representation, the appropriateness of which to the needed effect can be seen if we ask what we would not want Macbeth to do at this moment. We want him to be killed, as I have said, for his sake no less than that of Scotland; but we would not want him either to seek out Macduff or to flee the encounter when it comes or to "play the Roman fool"; we would not want him to show no recognition of the wrongs he has done Macduff or, when his last trust in the witches has gone, to continue to show fear or to yield or to fight with savage animosity; and he is made to do none of these things, but rather the contraries of all of them, so that he acts in the end as the Macbeth whose praises we have heard in the second scene of the play. And I would suggest that the cathartic effect of these words and acts is reinforced indirectly, in the representation, by the analogy we can hardly help drawing between his conduct now and the earlier conduct of young Siward, for of Macbeth too it can be said that "he parted well and paid his score"; the implication of this analogy is surely one of the functions, though not the only one, which the lines about Siward are intended to serve.

Charity and Grace

by G. R. Elliott

The question as to the central meaning of this drama turns upon the difference, not commonly recognized by the modern secular mind, between the true charity, which is *justly and righteously kind,* and that inadequate sort of charity which is the *milk* of human-kindness. The word milk, here as elsewhere in Shakespeare's works, is ambiguous: it may denote either nourishment or weakness, chiefly the latter in the case of Macbeth. But he is very typical; his conduct evinces both the potential value and the tragic limitation of that fellow-feeling, that human-kindness, which most people have most of the time. Ordinarily it serve to cement human society; but this cement melts very quickly, and for most persons surprisingly, in the heat of selfish interests. In vivid contrast is the virtuous charity of King Duncan, so carefully shown by the dramatist in the first Act. Unlike Macbeth, Duncan is not proudly conscious of his own kindness; in him it is a subordinate and nourishing constituent of the true charity. This king bears his faculties meekly and is clear in his great office, gentle but firm, mercifully just. He has the manly meekness that inherits the earth in the sense that it alone can transform human society into a real human family. And Shakespeare, with beautiful art, makes the spirit of Duncan persist throughout the play after his death, to become victorious at the close....

The whitest feature of Macbeth, however, is that, like his wife and unlike a multitude of other sinners, he does not strive to cloak his wickedness with conventional religiosity. Many a tyrant in pagan and Christian times, including Henry Eighth, has succeeded in conceiving his evil doings as in the main condoned by the gods or God. But Macbeth, with all his imagination, never imagines that. In the close of the play, for the first time in his career, he has to hear himself utterly condemned to his face for his wickedness: two noble gentlemen, Young Siward and Macduff, representing a wide range of human society, tell him plainly and strongly that he has become a servant of hell and the devil. And he does not utter a single word in repudiation of that verdict. So that our sense of uplift at the end of this tragedy is due in no small measure to the fact that Macbeth has at least the grace not to claim for his doings any tinge of Grace. And in this respect he adumbrates a characteristic of Shakespeare himself, who continually in his works shows up the hollowness and black deceptiveness of a merely conventional, egoistic piety.

A Reply to Cleanth Brooks

by Helen Gardner

A good example of the necessity of disciplining our imaginations and our responses by asking what associations the poet had in mind, rather than using the author's words as a starting-point for associations of our own, is a passage in *Macbeth* which was interpreted at some length by Professor Cleanth Brooks in *The Well-Wrought Urn*.[1] It can be shown that the critic has distorted the sense of the passage to make it an example of his general theory of the nature of poetry as distinct from prose. The interpretation he gives is shallower and less in keeping with the play as a whole than the interpretation we can arrive at by using Shakespeare to comment on Shakespeare. He isolates for discussion the lines where Macbeth "compares the pity for his victim-to-be, Duncan," to

> a naked new-born babe,
> Striding the blast, or heaven's cherubin, hors'd
> Upon the sightless couriers of the air...

and he comments as follows:

> The comparison is odd, to say the least. Is the babe natural or super-natural—an ordinary helpless baby, who, as newborn, could not, of course, even toddle, much less stride the blast? Or is it some infant Hercules, quite capable of striding the blast, but, since it is powerful and not helpless, hardly the typical pitiable object?
>
> Shakespeare seems bent upon having it both ways—and, if we read on through the passage—bent upon having the best of both worlds; for he proceeds to give us the option: pity is like the babe "or heaven's cherubim" who quite appropriately, of course, do ride the blast. Yet, even if we waive the question of the legitimacy of the alternative... is the cherubim comparison really any more successful than is the babe

[1]See pp. 38-39 in this volume.

comparison? Would not one of the great warrior archangels be more appropriate to the scene than the cherub? Does Shakespeare mean for pity or for fear of retribution to be dominant in Macbeth's mind?

Or was it possible that Shakespeare could not make up his own mind? Was he merely writing hastily and loosely, letting the word "pity" suggest the typically pitiable object, the babe naked in the blast, and then, stirred by the vague notion that some threat to Macbeth should be hinted, using "heaven's cherubim"—already suggested by "babe"—to convey the hint?

We know what the answer will be to all this puzzlement.[2] Shakespeare "meant for both." The passage is an example of the ambiguity, irony, paradox—the terms are roughly interchangeable—which Professor Brooks holds to be the differentiating quality of poetic speech. Later in the same essay the meaning is revealed:

> Pity is like the naked babe, the most sensitive and helpless thing, yet almost as soon as the comparison is announced, the symbol of weakness begins to turn into a symbol of strength; for the babe, though newborn, is pictured as "Striding the blast" like an elemental force—like "heaven's cherubim."...We can give an answer to the question put earlier: is Pity like the human and helpless babe, or powerful as the angel that rides the winds? It is both....The final and climactic appearance of the babe symbol merges all the contradictory elements of the symbol. For, with Macduff's statement about his birth, the naked babe rises before Macbeth as not only the future that eludes calculation but as avenging angel as well.

But why does Professor Brooks think that "heaven's cherubim" "quite appropriately ride the blast"? Why are they any more suitably imagined as "horsed" than the naked babe as "striding"? Why is it to be assumed that they imply "some threat to Macbeth"? Are cherubim to be thought of as powerful? Have we any reason to suppose that they should at once suggest to us the cliché "avenging angel"?

Most editors rightly cite here Psalm xviii, where the Lord is described descending in judgement: "He bowed the heavens also and came down: and it was dark under his feet. He rode upon the cherubims and did fly: he came flying upon the wings of the wind." Similarly, in Ezekiel's vision the cherubim are between the wheels of the chariot of the Lord; for the cherubim, in the visions of the Old Testa-

---

[2]It is a part of the game of "explication," as it has developed, to begin by expressing complete bafflement, as if the critic had never met a metaphor in his life. Then after every kind of obtuseness has been exhibited and all possible interpretations and misinterpretations have been considered, the true explication rises like the sun out of foggy mists.

ment, are the glory of the Lord, the signs of his presence. I do not
doubt that the association "cherubims"—"wings of the wind" helped
to create Shakespeare's lines. But there is no suggestion in the psalm,
although it is a psalm of judgement, that cherubim are avenging
angels. It is the Lord who is borne up by the cherubim; it is he that
flies on the wings of the wind. The cherubim are among the higher
orders of angels—the ministers who stand about the throne. They are
not the executors of God's purposes. They are with the Lord, whether
he comes in mercy or in judgement: "The Lord is King be the people
never so unpatient; he sitteth between the cherubims be the earth
never so unquiet." The cherubim, all gold and gilded over, carved at
the two ends of the mercy-seat, in the description of the covenant in
Exodus, are the tokens of the presence of the Lord among his people.

These are the cherubim of the Old Testament, Dionysius the Areo-
pagite, who established the hierarchy of the angels, the source of the
popular angelology of the Middle Ages, which the Elizabethans in-
herited, ranked the cherubim among the higher orders, as angels of
the presence. They stood about the throne, contemplating the glory
of God, not active, as were the lower orders, to fulfill his will on earth.
The cherubim glowed with knowledge, as the seraphim burned with
love. Hamlet, a scholarly character, glances at this learned conception
of the cherubim in his retort to Claudius:

> *Claudius.* So is it, if thou knew'st our purposes.
> *Hamlet.* I see a cherub that sees them.

Elsewhere, apart from two references to the gilded carvings of cherubim, Shakespeare appears to use the word in its popular sense, to
signify primarily beauty, particularly the radiant and innocent beauty
of youth. Thus we may have the word used, as in Sonnet 114, for a
simple opposite to the hideous:

> To make of monsters and things indigest
> Such cherubins as your sweet self resemble.

Or the idea of youthfulness is stressed, as in *The Merchant of Venice:*

> Still quiring to the young-eyed cherubins.

or the idea of innocence, as in *Timon of Athens:*

> This fell whore of thine
> Hath in her more destruction than thy sword
> For all her cherubin look.

But in two plays, one written just before, the other some time after *Macbeth,* Shakespeare gives this innocent youthful beauty a certain moral colouring which is, as far as I know, his own; at least I have not met with it in another writer. In the late play, *The Tempest,* Prospero tells Miranda how he was set adrift with her when she was a baby, and she exclaims

> Alack! what trouble
> Was I then to you.

But he answers:

> O, a cherubin
> Thou wast, that did preserve me! Thou didst smile,
> Infused with a fortitude from heaven,
> When I have deck'd the sea with drops full salt,
> Under my burden groan'd; which rais'd in me
> An undergoing stomach, to bear up
> Against what should ensue.

Because Prospero sees the three-year-old Miranda as a cherub, smiling and giving him patience to bear up, I find no difficulty in taking Othello's cry "Patience, thou young and rose-lipped cherubin!" as an apostrophe to a virtue which Shakespeare elsewhere pictures as radiantly young and beautiful. In the recognition scene of *Pericles,* Pericles, gazing on his exquisite young daughter, who claims that she has endured "a grief might equal yours," wonders at her endurance, for, he exclaims,

> thou dost look
> Like Patience gazing on kings' graves, and smiling
> Extremity out of act.

Although Viola's description of her sister, "like Patience on a monument, smiling at grief," is often cited to prove that Shakespeare could not have thought of Patience as "young and rose-lipped," since Viola's sister had lost her damask cheek and had pined in thought,[3] the passage in *Pericles* admits of no doubt. It plainly implies a beauty un-

---

[3]This is absurdly supported by some commentators by reference to Nym's "Patience is a tired nag." There has been much discussion as to whether Shakespeare had a particular monument in mind. Although none has been discovered to fit the description, I think, in spite of their being far apart in time, we must take both Viola's and Pericles' words as referring to the same conception. Because Viola's sister lost her beauty, we need not take it that Shakespeare means us to think of the virtue which she exemplifies as pale and worn. She is like Patience on a monument in that she "smiles at grief."

touched by care. In *Othello* then, written just before *Macbeth,* and in
The Tempest, written some time after, a cherub is thought of as not
only young, beautiful, and innocent, but as associated with the virtue
of patience, conceived of as an endurance which is not grim, but
heavenly, smiling, and serene. It could, however, be objected at this
point that because Shakespeare elsewhere invariably sees the cherubim as young and beautiful, and conceives them as particularly associated with the bearing of wrong rather than with the avenging of it,
we cannot assume that he never saw them otherwise. Although there is
no support for the idea in Scripture or in popular angelology, and no
parallel elsewhere in his works, he might, in this passage, because of
a confused memory of Psalm xviii, conceive of cherubim as avengers
threatening Macbeth; for there is apocalyptic imagery just before in
the simile of the accusing "angels trumpet-tongu'd."

The context is our final test. Macbeth, having acknowledged the
certainty of retribution in this life, that "we still have judgement
here," goes on to give the reasons which make the deed which he is
meditating peculiarly base. It is the murder of a kinsman and a king,
who is also a guest who trusts his host to protect him:

> Besides, this Duncan
> Hath borne his faculties so meek, hath been
> So clear in his great office, that his virtues
> Will plead like angels trumpet-tongu'd against
> The deep damnation of his taking off;
> And pity, like a naked new-born babe,
> Striding the blast, or heaven's cherubin, hors'd
> Upon the sightless couriers of the air,
> Shall blow the horrid deed in every eye,
> That tears shall drown the wind.

The final image of the wind dropping as the rain begins is the termina-
tion of the whole sequence of ideas and images. It is to this close that
they hurry. The passage ends with tears stilling the blast. The final
condemnation of the deed is not that it will meet with punishment,
not even that the doer of it will stand condemned; but that even
indignation at the murder will be swallowed up in universal pity for
the victim. The whole world will know, and knowing it will not curse
but weep. The babe, naked and new-born, the most helpless of all
things, the cherubim, innocent and beautiful, call out the pity and the
love by which Macbeth is judged. It is not terror of heaven's vengeance
which makes him pause; but the terror of moral isolation. He ends by
seeing himself alone in a sudden silence, where nothing can be heard

but weeping, as, when a storm has blown itself out, the wind drops and we hear the steady falling of the rain, which sounds as if it would go on for ever. The naked babe "strides the blast" because pity is to Shakespeare the strongest and profoundest of human emotions, the distinctively human emotion. It rises above and masters indignation. The cherubim are borne with incredible swiftness about the world because the virtues of Duncan are of such heavenly beauty that they command universal love and reverence. He has "borne his faculties so meek" and been "so clear in his great office." The word "clear" is a radiant word, used by Shakespeare elsewhere of the Gods. The helplessness of the king who has trusted him, his gentle virtues, and patient goodness are transformed in Macbeth's mind into the most helpless of all things, what most demands our protection, and then into what awake tenderness, love, and reverence. The babe merges into the cherubim, not because Shakespeare means Macbeth to be feeling both pity and fear of retribution at the same time, but because Shakespeare, like Keats, believes in "the holiness of the heart's affections."

In a very early play, in a savage scene full of curses and cries for vengeance, Shakespeare uses the same natural image as he does here. In Henry VI, part 3, Margaret, having crowned York with a paper crown, hands him a napkin dipped in his little son's blood, and York exclaims

> Bidd'st thou me rage? why, now thou hast thy wish;
> Would'st have me weep? why, now thou hast thy will;
> For raging wind blows up incessant showers,
> And when the rage allays, the rain begins.

And in his next speech he prophesies that Margaret's deed will have the same condemnation as Macbeth forsees for his:

> Keep thou the napkin, and go boast of this;
> And if thou tell'st the heavy story right,
> Upon my soul, the hearers will shed tears;
> Yea, even my foes will shed fast-falling tears,
> And say, "Alas! it was a piteous deed."

This seems feeble enough, and yet it holds the characteristic Shakespearian appeal to our deepest moral feelings. The worst suffering is to suffer alone; it is more comfort to York in his agony to think that common humanity will make even his enemies weep with him than to think of vengeance on the murderess of his son. Professor Brooks has sacrificed this Shakespearian depth of human feeling, visible even in this crude early play, by attempting to interpret an image by the aid of what associations it happens to arouse in him, and by being more interested in making symbols of babes fit each other than in listening to what Macbeth is saying. *Macbeth* is a tragedy and not a melodrama or a symbolic drama of retribution. The reappearance of "the babe symbol" in the apparition scene and in Macduff's revelation of his birth has distracted the critic's attention from what deeply moves the imagination and the conscience in this vision of a whole world weeping at the inhumanity of helplessness betrayed and innocence and beauty destroyed. It is the judgement of the human heart that Macbeth fears here, and the punishment which the speech foreshadows is not that he will be cut down by Macduff, but that having murdered his own humanity he will enter into a world of appalling loneliness, of meaningless activity, unloved himself, and unable to love.

Macbeth

by L. C. Knights

Some years ago Professor Oscar James Campbell, in an essay called, "Shakespeare and the 'New' Critics,"[1] discussed what seemed to him the ill-founded assumption that intensive analysis of imagery might lead to the discovery of a play's "inner imaginative structure." I am not concerned here with the justice or otherwise of his observations on particular pieces of work by two critics—they were Cleanth Brooks and D. A. Traversi—but only with the grounds of his disagreement from them. These are, I think, fairly indicated by the following:

> The principle reason for the failure of these interpreters...[is that] they approach each play of Shakespeare under a compulsion to find in his poetry those characteristics which T. S. Eliot and his followers have decided must be present in all pure poetry. They assume therefore that Shakespeare, like Donne, constructed an integrated system of connotation based on the iteration of certain words, to which the poet had given an arbitrary symbolical value. And they make the further assumption that in this system of sequence and repetition of images all the poetry of the play is fused into one intense impression.
>
> But Shakespeare seems never to have manipulated his imagery in this consciously scheming fashion. His poetry rather gives the effect of a spontaneous eruption from that secret region of the mind where the imaginative impulse is generated. His imagination usually finds release, not in an integrated structure of figures, but rather in a medley of metaphors, each one relevant only to some specific emotional situation....
>
> The truth is [Professor Campbell concludes] that Shakespeare employed his images for two purposes, both dramatic. He made his figura-

---

[1]See pp. 54-59 ff. in this volume.

tive language intensify an auditor's response to particular situations
and also used it to create and individualize his characters.

That, apart from a suggestion that imagery helps to create "mood,"
is all that is allowed to the imagery of a Shakespeare play: to attempt
to find more in it is to stray into "the wasteland of paradox, ambiguity,
and esoteric symbolism."

If we feel that observations such as these are not critically useful,
that they are blurred and out of focus, how can we justify alternative
critical principles that give due recognition to precisely those elements
that Professor Campbell seems bent on excluding?[2]

It is the function of imagery that Professor Campbell is mainly
concerned with. Let us take one of his own examples. He refers us to
Lady Macbeth's words to her husband, —

> I have given suck, and know
> How tender 'tis to love the babe that milks me:
> I would, while it was smiling in my face,
> Have pluck'd my nipple from his boneless gums,
> And dash'd the brains out, had I so sworn as you
> Have done to this.

This, we are told, has a "stark simplicity....What she says to her
husband is this: Rather than be such an irresolute coward as you now
are, I had rather be guilty of the most fiendishly unnatural deed of
which a mother is capable." Well, she does say that. But is that all she
says? We can, at all events, hardly fail to be impressed by the violence
of the image, and we may legitimately regard the violence of tone as a
part of the meaning of what Lady Macbeth says. The play, after all, is
about a succession of violent acts—culminating in the murder of Macduff's babes—which are continually reflected in violent imagerys "to
bathe in reeking wounds," "even till destruction sicken," and so on.
But the particular choice of image in Lady Macbeth's speech surely
does more than this. It is not only an image of violence, but of unnatural violence, and thus links with the insistence on "unnatural
deeds" so pervasive throughout the play that illustration is unneces-
sary. And the violence expressed by Lady Macbeth is directed not
only towards others but towards herself. She is attempting, as she bids

---

[2]It is of course true, as Professor Campbell contends, that Shakespeare did not give
"an arbitrary symbolical value" to certain words; nor did he "manipulate" his imagery in
a "consciously scheming fashion." Since I have quoted from this essay for my own purposes it is only fair to add that its intention—to insist that Shakespeare's "comprehen-
siveness and complexity" should not be racked to fit a preconceived scheme—is entirely
laudable.

her husband a moment later, to "screw her courage to the sticking-place"; and this—like Macbeth's

> I am settled, and *bend up*
> Each corporal agent to this terrible feat—

evokes an unnatural tension of the will ("I have no spur/ To prick the sides of my intent...") which is certainly part of the play's dramatic substance, whatever our views about the nature of poetic drama. The lines, in short, *reverberate,* and there is a process of what I. A. Richards calls interinanimation between the image on which we are focusing and some scores of others throughout the play. And this, surely, is one of the ways in which the poetic mind works when fully engaged at the deepest levels.

We may push our enquiry a little further. When does imagery exercise this mutually attractive power, which issues in something not merely relevant to character or the immediate situation? When we enlist in our interpretation of a Shakespearean tragedy a pattern of imagery, what guarantee have we that we are not behaving in an arbitrary fashion? To this last question a short answer, and in the end the only one, is that our only safeguard is our own ability to read poetry: lacking that we can play any wilful tricks we like, and foist on Shakespeare, or any other dramatist, such schematic interpretations as our ingenuity can construct. But rational argument consists in expanding short answers into longer ones, and I return to my question.

In the fifth act of *King John,* when the King is dying and the revolted English lords are about to return to their allegiance, these lines occur:

> But even this night, whose black contagious breath
> Already smokes about the burning crest
> Of the old, feeble and day-wearied sun....

In the third act of *Macbeth,* when Macbeth has planned the murder of Banquo, we have these lines:

> Light thickens; and the crow
> Makes wing to th' rooky wood;
> Good things of Day begin to droop and drowse....

If I claim that the first of these extracts merely embellishes the particular situation,[3] but that the second forms part of a larger pattern

---

[3]Dr. Tillyard says: "'contagious' (suggesting sickness) and the sun combine to indicate the King's present sickness through poison" (*Shakespeare's History Plays,* p. 219). If I disagree with this it is for the reasons indicated in the remainder of the paragraph.

that lies behind the plot and the characters, on what grounds should I base my distinction? The lines from Macbeth are of course more compressed and more striking: "light *thickens*" has an element of surprise which is lacking in the trope about night's "black contagious breath." And in the two and a half lines from *Macbeth* there is more *going on* than in the three lines from *King John*. Not only is the coming on of night vividly evoked, and with it a sensation of moral torpor, but the enclosed image of the crow returning to its nest introduces an extra vibration as the murderer momentarily follows its tranquil customary flight—as customary and secure as the building and breeding of the temple-haunting martlets.[4] And this, of course, is not all. In *Macbeth* previous images of darkness and of torpor have helped to determine the way in which we receive the quoted passage when it comes. Yet—and this brings me to my main point—if *King John* were full of images similar to the one I have quoted I should not feel that there was a significance in that play beyond the significance of its overt political theme. You cannot discuss imagery apart from the living tissue of which it forms a part. *King John* is a good play, containing some admirably vigorous poetry; but the kind of attention that its poetry demands is qualitatively different from the kind of attention demanded by the poetry of *Macbeth*. And the level at which meanings take place in poetry is determined by the kind and degree of activity that the poetry—the whole play—calls for on the part of the reader. Not only is the verse of *Macbeth* more fluid, more vivid and compressed than the verse of *King John,* the mind of the reader or spectator is more fully activated, and activated in different ways. The compression, the thick clusters of imagery (with rapidly changing metaphors completely superseding the similes and drawn-out figures to be found in the earlier plays), the surprising juxtapositions, the over-riding of grammar, and the shifts and overlapping of meanings— all these, demanding an unusual liveliness of attention, force the reader to respond with the whole of his active imagination.

It is only when the mind of the reader is thoroughly "roused and awakened,"[5] that meanings from below the level of "plot" and "character" take form as a living structure. If that structure of meaning seems especially closely connected with recurring and inter-related imagery, that is not because possible associations and recurrences are puzzled out by the intellect, but because the mind at a certain pitch

---

[4]W. Empson has some other interesting suggestions concerning the uncanny "atmosphere" of these lines. See *Seven Types of Ambiguity* (1930), pp. 23-25.

[5]The reference to Chapter XV of the *Biographia Literaria* is deliberate.

of activity and responsiveness combines the power of focusing lucidly on what is before it with an awareness of before and after, sensing the whole in the part, and with a triumphant energy relating part to part in a living whole. But it is only in relation to that larger all-embracing meaning—determined by the "plain sense" of what is said, and by its overtones, by the dramatic situation and the progress of the action, by symbols and by the interplay of different attitudes embodied in the different persons of the drama—it is only in relation to this total meaning that the imagery, or any other component that may be momentarily isolated, takes on its full significance. We only hear Shakespeare's deeper meanings when we listen with the whole of ourselves. ...

Macbeth defines a particular kind of evil—the evil that results from a lust for power. The defining, as in all the tragedies, is in strictly poetic and dramatic terms. It is certainly not an abstract formulation, but lies rather in the drawing out of necessary consequences and implications of that lust both in the external and the spiritual worlds. Its meaning, therefore, is revealed in the expansion and unfolding of what lies within the initial evil, in terms of direct human experience. The logic is not formal but experiential, and demands from us, if we are to test its validity and feel its force, a fulness of imaginative response and a closeness of realization, in which both sensation and feeling become modes of understanding. Only when intellect, emotion, and a kind of direct sensory awareness work together can we enter fully into that exploratory and defining process.

In other words, the essential structure of *Macbeth*, as of the other tragedies, is to be sought in the poetry. That of course is easily said; what it means is something that can only be grasped in relation to specific instances or not grasped at all. We may take as an example Macbeth's "aside" when he has been greeted as Thane of Cawdor.

> This supernatural soliciting
> Cannot be ill; cannot be good:—
> If ill, why hath it given me earnest of success,
> Commencing in a truth? I am thane of Cawdor:
> If good, why do I yield to that suggestion
> Whose horrid image doth unfix my hair,
> And make my seated heart knock at my ribs,
> Against the use of nature? Present fears
> Are less than horrible imaginings.
> My thought, whose murder yet is but fantastical,

> Shakes so my single state of man,
> That function is smother'd in surmise,
> And nothing is, but what is not.   (I. iii. 130-42)

This is temptation, presented with concrete force. Even if we attend
only to the revelation of Macbeth's spiritual state, our recognition of
the body—the very feel—of the experience, is a response to the poetry,
to such things as the sickening see-saw rhythm ("Cannot be ill; cannot
be good...") changing to the rhythm of the pounding heart, the over-
riding of grammar ("My thought, whose murder yet is but fantastical")
as thought is revealed in the very process of formation, and so on. But
the poetry makes further claims, and if we attend to them we find that
the words do not only point inward to the presumed state of Macbeth's
mind but, as it were, outward to the play as a whole. The equivocal
nature of temptation, the commerce with phantoms consequent upon
false choice, the resulting sense of unreality ("nothing is, but what is
not"), which has yet such power to "smother" vital function, the unnaturalness of evil ("against the use of nature"), and the relation
between disintegration in the individual ("my single state of man")
and disorder in the larger social organism—all these are major themes
of the play which are mirrored in the speech under consideration.
They emerge as themes because they are what the poetry—reinforced
by action and symbolism—again and again insists on. And the interrelations we are forced to make take us outside the speeches of the
protagonist to the poetry of the play as a whole. That "smother'd," for
example, takes us forward not only to Lady Macbeth's "blanket of the
dark" but to such things as Rosse's choric comment after the murder
of Duncan:—

> by th' clock 'tis day,
> And yet dark night strangles the travelling lamp.
> Is't night's predominance, or the day's shame,
> That darkness does the face of earth entomb,
> When living light should kiss it?   (II. iv. 6-10)

In none of the tragedies is there anything superfluous, but it is
perhaps *Macbeth* that gives the keenest impression of economy. The
action moves directly and quickly to the crisis, and from the crisis
to the full working out of plot and theme. The pattern is far easier
to grasp than that of *Lear*. The main theme of the reversal of values
is given out simply and clearly in the first scene—"Fair is foul, and
foul is fair"; and with it are associated premonitions of the conflict,
disorder and moral darkness into which Macbeth will plunge himself.

Well before the end of the first act we are in possession not only of the positive values against which the Macbeth evil will be defined but of the related aspects of that evil, which is simultaneously felt as a strained and unnatural perversion of the will, an obfuscation of the clear light of reason, a principle of disorder (both in the "single state of man" and in his wider social relations), and a pursuit of illusions. All these impressions, which as the play proceeds assume the status of organizing ideas, are produced by the inter-action of all the resources of poetic drama—action, contrast, statement, implication, imagery and allusion. Thus the sense of the unnaturalness of evil is evoked not only by repeated explicit references ("nature's mischief," "nature seems dead," " 'Tis unnatural, even like the deed that's done," and so on) but by the expression of unnatural sentiments and an unnatural violence of tone in such things as Lady Macbeth's invocation of the "spirits" who will "unsex" her, and her affirmation that she would murder the babe at her breast if she had sworn to do it. So too the theme of the false appearances inseparable from evil, of deceit recoiling on the deceiver, is not only the subject of explicit comment

> And be these juggling fiends no more believ'd,
> That palter with us in a double sense   (V. viii. 19-20)

it is embodied in the action, so that Macbeth's despairing recognition of mere "mouth-honour" among his remaining followers (V. iii. 27) echoes ironically his wife's advice to "look like th' innocent flower, But be the serpent under't" (I. v. 64-65) and the hypocritical play of the welcoming of Duncan; and it is reinforced by—or indeed one with —the evoked sense of equivocation and evasiveness associated with the witches, and the cloud of uncertainty that settles on Scotland during Macbeth's despotism. It is fitting that the final movement of the reversal that takes place in the last act should open with the command of Malcolm to the camouflaged soldiers, "Your leavy screens throw down,/ And show like those you are" (V. vi. 1-2).

II

The assurance of *Macbeth* has behind it, is indeed based on, a deeply imagined resolution of perplexities inherent in any full exposure to life. Freedom from the tyranny of time and illusion is finally related, at the deepest levels of consciousness, to the central affirmations of the spirit; and conversely, the obsessed awareness of time without meaning, like the subjection of mind to appearance, is revealed not simply as consequential on false choice but as intrinsic to it: for "the eye altering alters all." There is a similar assurance in the use of "nature," in that aspect of the play's imaginative structure that impels us to say not merely that Macbeth's crime is unnatural (i.e., inhuman) but that the values against which evil is defined are in some sense grounded in nature. To suggest how this is so, to relate the insights operative here to those already touched on, it is necessary to step back from the play and to see it in the wider context of Shakespeare's development as a whole. Although in recent years much has been written about the meanings of nature in Shakespeare and his contemporaries, there is still need for further clarification of the perceptions controlling the use of this elusive, indispensable and pregnant word.

In Shakespeare's poetic thought we find two apparently contradictory intuitions regarding man's relation to the created world existing independently of human choice and will. Nature and human values are felt as intimately related, and at the same time as antagonistic.

They are related in two ways. Shakespeare, like almost all poets, uses natural imagery to evoke and define qualities that are humanly valuable, indeed indispensable to any full humanity:

> She that herself will sliver and disbranch
> From her material sap, perforce must wither
> And come to deadly use.

>   For his bounty,
> There was no winter in't; an autumn 'twas
> That grew the more by reaping.

These are striking instances, but in even apparently casual metaphors and similes—"my love is all as boundless as the sea," "and she in thee/ Calls back the lovely April of her prime," "as dear to me as are the ruddy drops/ That visit my sad heart"—it seems that we have to do with a relationship more intimate than that of mere resemblance: the mind has in some sense *found itself* in nature; for, as Leone Vivante says of Shakespeare's images of budding and of morning, "the grace of things in their birth and their first purity would not be perceived, if it were not *first* a quality of our mental synthesis which is revealed in and through them."[6] This is indeed a truth of general application; Blake's Tiger, Herbert's Flower, Marvell's Garden (in the poems of those names), and Wordsworth's

---

[6]Leone Vivante, *English Poetry and its Contribution to the Knowledge of a Creative Principle,* p. 18. See also Coleridge, "On Poesy or Art," *Biographia Literaria,* ed. Shaw-cross. Vol. II, pp. 257-58.

> uncertain heaven, received
> Into the bosom of the steady lake,   (*The Prelude*, V. 387-88)

all imply a basic kinship of human and non-human life: mind would be less truly itself if it were not deeply responsive to images such as these. The correspondences between mind and natural forms and natural processes is attested by common speech as well as by the poets. Just as it is with peculiar rightness that George Herbert can say, "And now in age I bud again," or that Marvell can speak of "a green thought in a green shade," so images of budding, growing, harvesting, of night, dawn and day, of seasons and weathers, of climates and landscapes, are integral to the speech in which we ourselves feel after inner experience.

> La Nature est un temple où de vivants piliers
> Laissent parfois sortir de confuses paroles;
> L'homme y passe à travers des forêts de symboles
> Qui l'observent avec des regards familiers.[7]

In Shakespeare there is no attempt to explain the working of these *regards familiers;* but the mere fact that his plays and poems are full of these more-than-analogies implies that psychic life is at home in nature.

But even if we leave aside the difficult question of natural symbolism, there is no doubt that wherever Shakespeare envisages a fully human way of life he thinks of it as closely related to the wider setting of organic growth, as indeed, in a quite concrete and practical way, directly based on man's dealings with the earth that nourishes him. It is of course in *The Winter's Tale* that we are most explicitly aware of nature as a powerful controlling presence[8]—a presence moreover not vaguely felt but specifically rendered in the great pastoral scene with its many reminders of seasonal activities, humble in themselves but translucent to the great myths. But Shakespeare's vision of the intimate relationship between man and nature, of nature as the necessary basis and, under certain conditions, the pattern for civilization, goes back to the period before the final plays and before the tragedies. It is expressed in the beautiful but strangely neglected speech of Burgundy, in *King Henry V,* when he urges peace.

---

[7]Baudelaire, "Correspondences." That Baudelaire goes on from this fine opening to discuss questions of synaesthesia is perhaps unfortunate but irrelevant.

[8]Wilson Knight, in his perceptive study of the play "'Great Creating Nature'" *(The Crown of Life),* speaks of it as "an all-powerful presence, at once controller and exemplar." But even for nature in *The Winter's Tale* "all-powerful" is not precisely the right adjective.

>   ...let it not disgrace me
> If I demand before this royal view,
> Why that the naked, poor, and mangled Peace,
> Dear nurse of arts, plenties, and joyful births,
> Should not in this best garden of the world,
> Our fertile France, put up her lovely visage?
> Alas! she hath from France too long been chas'd,
> And all her husbandry doth lie on heaps,
> Corrupting in its own fertility.
> Her vine, the merry cheerer of the heart,
> Unpruned dies; her hedges even-pleach'd
> Like prisioners wildly overgrown with hair,
> Put forth disorder'd twigs; her fallow leas
> The darnel, hemlock and rank fumitory
> Doth root upon, while that the coulter rusts
> That should deracinate such savagery;
> The even mead, that erst brought sweetly forth
> The freckled cowslip, burnet, and green clover,
> Wanting the scythe, all uncorrected, rank,
> Conceives by idleness, and nothing teems
> But hateful docks, rough thistles, kecksies, burrs,
> Losing both beauty and utility.
> And as our vineyards, fallows, meads, and hedges,
> Defective in their natures, grow to wildness,
> Even so our houses and ourselves and children
> Have lost, or do not learn for want of time,
> The sciences that should become our country,
> But grow like savages, as soldiers will
> That nothing do but meditate on blood,
> To swearing and stern looks, defus'd attire,
> And every thing that seems unnatural.   (V. ii. 31-62)

There is here an imaginative vision that transcends the simple sequence of the argument. After the preliminary invocation of peace
the passage is built on a simple inversion: uncultivated nature ("cor-
rupting in its own fertility"—a phrase that Milton must have remem-
bered) is compared to disorderly or uncultivated human life, which in
turn is compared to "wild" or "savage" nature. But what we have to
deal with is something more complex than a simple comparison
which is then given again with the terms reversed; Burgundy is
throughout expressing a sense of the interrelationship—a two-way
traffic—between man and nature. Natural fertility ("our fertile France")

is the necessary precondition not only of life at the biological level but of the highest reaches of man-made civilization—the "arts" and "sciences" (both of which can be interpreted in the widest sense); whilst at the same time, since peace is the nurse not only of these but of all that comes to birth, of the very fertility on which the whole range of human activity depends, and since it is man who *makes* peace, man is responsible for nature. The alternative to peace is "wildness" in both man and nature, and for man to tame that wildness in himself is a process analogous to taming what is given in external nature. So much is stated or directly suggested: what is not quite explicit but imaginatively present, adding life and vibrancy to the flat prose-meaning to which I have reduced the poetry, is the vision of peace. Conceived throughout as a wholesome *activity*—"laying" hedges, ploughing, and so on are taken as representative examples—it is a state in which arts and sciences and daily beauty and utility are conceived both as end and as condition of the fertility on which all alike depend. Behind the image of life and nature run wild for lack of human care is the implied ideal of natural force tended and integrated into a truly human civilization. And the inclusive "Peace," teeming with human activity, is the "natural" end of the "joyful births": it is the alternative "wildness" that is "unnatural."

But if Burgundy's speech, looking forward as it does to *The Winter's Tale,* represents an important element in Shakespeare's imaginative vision of man and nature, there is also another, its polar opposite, of which a brief reminder will serve. If nature is bounty she is also decay; she is the ally of chance in "untrimming" "every fair" (Sonnet XVIII); it is the same sky that indifferently "cheers" and "checks" both men and flowers (Sonnet XV). Worse still, if nature as the world of organic growth and decay is indifferent to human needs, as instinct and appetite ("blood") she can be positively hostile to the life of the spirit. And between "natural law" as traditionally understood (*i.e.,* reason) and the law of nature by which, as Falstaff lightly remarked, the young dace is a bait for the old pike, there is an absolute distinction.

All this Shakespeare knew well enough, and in *King Lear,* addressing himself to the question of man's place in nature, and with a full view of all the potential evil in man as part of nature, he magnificently re-affirmed the autonomy of the spirit. Yet in Shakespeare's poetic thought the idea of relationship to nature seems as integral as the idea of the fundamental difference between the two realms. The question we are forced to ask, therefore, is, If human nature is not entirely at home in the world of nature, if in some essential ways it is set over against nature, how can mind find itself in nature, as there is such abundant testimony that it does? How is it that in *Macbeth* (to be specific) essential distinctions of good and evil, belonging to the inner world, can be defined in imagery of the outer world of nature, defined moreover in such a way that the imaginative correspondence goes far beyond the use of selected analogies and implies a symbolic equivalence—indeed a relationship—between what is "natural" for man and what is "natural" in the simplest and widest sense of the word?[9]

We are led back once more to *King Lear,* to one scene in particular where we first become conscious of a change in direction of the imaginative current of the play, as though a slight but unmistakable breeze were announcing that a tide, still at the ebb, is about to turn. In the opening scenes of Act IV the worst is still to come; both Gloucester and Lear have still to reach the lowest point of their despair. But Gloucester, we know, is in the care of Edgar, and in the fourth scene, immediately after we have been told of Lear's purgatorial shame, Cordelia enters, "with drum and colours," seeking her father.

> *Cordelia.* Alack! 'tis he: why, he was met even now
> As mad as the vex'd sea; singing aloud;
> Crown'd with rank fumiter and furrow-weeds,
> With hardocks, hemlock, nettles, cuckoo-flowers,
> Darnel, and all the idle weeds that grow
> In our sustaining corn. A century send forth;
> Search every acre in the high-grown field,
> And bring him to our eye. [*Exit* an officer.]
>   What can man's wisdom
> In the restoring his bereaved sense?
> He that helps him take all my outward worth.
> *Doctor.* There is means, madam;
> Our foster-nurse of nature is repose,
> The which he lacks; that to provoke in him,
> Are many simples operative, whose power
> Will close the eye of anguish.
> *Cordelia.*   All bless'd secrets,
> All you unpublish'd virtues of the earth,

[9]It is of course common for good and evil to be compared respectively to beneficent and harmful or unpleasant aspects of nature,—as we might speak of bounty as a harvest or miserliness as a black frost. But in *Macbeth* analogies for human good are found in the *general* process of nature, whereas evil is defined solely in terms of what is perverse or abnormal in nature, and is constantly described as "'gainst nature" or "unnatural." Nature, we are made to feel, is on the side of good and disowns evil. See Wilson Knight's essay on "Life-Themes in *Macbeth,*" in *The Imperial Theme.*

> Spring with my tears! be aidant and remediate
> In the good man's distress! Seek, seek for him,
> Lest his ungovern'd rage dissolve the life
> That wants the means to lead it.   (IV. iv. 1-20)

What is remarkable here is the particular quality of the awareness of nature that lies behind and informs the poetry. Lear's "ungovern'd rage" is compared, as before, to elemental fury ("as mad as the vex'd sea"), and his mock crown is fittingly made up of "idle weeds," astonishingly present in the clogged movement of the lines that list them. Yet co-present with these—and given emphasis by the lift and smooth sweep of the verse—is "our sustaining corn"; and the same earth bears the medicinal plants that foster restoring sleep ("balm of hurt minds, great nature's second course").[10] Nature, then, is contemplated in both its aspects, as that which preserves and as that which impedes, encroaches on or rises in turmoil against man's specifically human activities; and it is contemplated with a peculiar serenity. It is of course contemplated from the standpoint of Cordelia; and her qualities—those particularly that lie behind this serenity—have been explicitly and beautifully evoked in the immediately preceding scene. The law of her nature, it is clear, is quite other than the law of nature to which Goneril and Regan abandon themselves:—

> it seem'd she was a queen
> Over her passion; who, most rebel-like,
> Sought to be king o'er her.   (IV. iii. 14-16)

Yet there is nothing rigid in this self-control. She is mov'd, though

---

[10]It is indeed impossible to make a sharp distinction between harmful "weeds" and beneficent "simples." According to the notes in Professor Muir's Arden edition, fumitory "was formerly employed in cases of hypochondrism and black jaundice," darnel has narcotic powers, and hemlock is used as a narcotic as well as a poison. Compare Friar Lawrence's soliloquy, in *Romeo and Juliet*, II, iii, on earth's "baleful weeds and precious-juiced flowers,"—

> Many for many virtues excellent,
> None but for some, and yet all different...
> For nought so vile that on the earth doth live
> But to the earth some special good doth give;
> Nor aught so good but, strain'd from that fair use,
> Revolts from true birth, stumbling on abuse...
> Two such opposed kings encamp them still
> In man as well as herbs, grace and rude will. ...

This passage is quoted in Edgar C. Knowlton's "Nature and Shakespeare" (*P.M.L.A.*, LI, 1936, pp. 718 ff.), which sees Shakespeare's conception of Nature in relation to traditional thought, and lists many interesting passages.

"not to a rage"; and we feel it fitting that one so far removed from all
that is merely natural should yet attract to herself images and associations from the world of nature,

> ...patience and sorrow strove
> Who should express her goodliest. You have seen
> Sunshine and rain at once; her smiles and tears
> Were like, a better way,   (IV. iii. 18-20)

just as it is perfectly in keeping that religious associations—"There
she shook/ The holy water from her heavenly eyes" (IV. iii. 30-31)—
should almost immediately blend with those of "sunshine and rain at
once."[11] What we are given in the poetry is a sure and sensitive poise,
and it is Cordelia's integrity—her tenderness, as we have seen, at one
with her strength—that explains her full and ready responsiveness. It
is because she is fully human—though there are also potent suggestions of divine grace—that she is "natural" in a different sense from
that intended in Edmund's philosophy. Her sense of the bounty of
nature (of "our sustaining corn" as well as of the "rank fumiter and
furrow-weeds") lies behind her invocation,—

> All bless'd secrets,
> All you unpublish'd virtues of the earth,
> Spring with my tears! be aidant and remediate
> In the good man's distress!

But it is because of her love and pity ("the good man" is the erring
Lear) that she can invoke so whole-heartedly the "unpublish'd virtues
of the earth"—can invoke them moreover not simply as allies from a
different realm, but with a suggestion of kinship and intimacy that
almost equates their working with the power of out-going and healing
life that lies deep in the soul.[12] It is in this sense that Cordelia "redeems nature from the general curse/ Which twain have brought her
to" (IV. vi. 207-208).

It is this complex resolution of feeling, issuing in new insight, that

[11]D. A. Traversi discusses the complex imagery of this passage in his *Approach to
Shakespeare* (p. 78), and in his chapter on Shakespeare's last plays in the Pelican *Guide
to English Literature, 2, The Age of Shakespeare* (p. 258).

[12]It is, I think, in the injunction, "Spring with my tears," that Shakespeare establishes
the close kinship of human nature and the wider nature from which it is born. Taken by
itself, of course, the phrase is not particularly remarkable; it is only in its context that it
has this subtle force of suggestion. But there seems no end to the subtle interrelation-
ships of imagery in *King Lear*. Thus one has only to linger on the adjective "unpublish'd" to see its small but significant part in the counter-movement of the play. Elsewhere the emphasis is on hidden corruption, "what plighted cunning hides," "undi-
vulged crimes," and so on. But there are also "bless'd secrets" and "unpublish'd virtues."

lies behind the use of "nature" in *Macbeth*. Since the insight stems from a mode of being and is inseparable from it, it cannot be summed up in a formula. But in matters of this kind simple formulations have their uses, if only as a way of ensuring that necessary complexity has not, in the course of argument, degenerated into mere verbal complication, or that mountains are not being made out of molehills. Shakespeare, then, does not say that "nature, however inscrutable, is basically beneficent"; he does not say that there is "in nature a core of tenderness, which lies even deeper than pride or cruelty."[13] He says—though it takes the whole of *King Lear* to say it adequately—that nature *per se* is something quite other than human nature, and that it cannot properly be conceived in human terms; that its humanly relevant quality only exists in relation to a particular human outlook and standpoint; and that what that quality is depends on the standpoint from which the relation is established. "Nature-as-beneficent" is a concept that only has meaning for the good man—or at all events for the man who admits the imperatives of his own humanity. Perhaps it is easier to grasp this in relation to the world—the given "nature"—of inner experience. The mind ("that ocean, where each kind/ Does straight its own resemblance find") contains within itself elements corresponding to non-human life—Blake's tiger and lamb. So long as these natural forces are not integrated by the specifically human principle they are, or are likely to become, chaotic and destructive. Given that principle, they may be sublimated and transformed, but they are not disowned: they are freely accepted as the natural sources of life and power.[14] So too with the external world of nature: it is only the man who recog-

---

[13]"The main element in Jacobean pessimism had been the conviction that evil, including its destructive potentialities, was natural. ...But the dominant theme of *Macbeth*, a theme reiterated by all the leading characters and in most of the major scenes, is that evil is unnatural. Nature, however inscrutable, is basically beneficent, and such a crime as Macbeth's is not in accordance with nature but contrary to it."—H. B. Parkes, "Nature's Diverse Laws: the Double Vision of the Elizabethans" (*The Sewanee Review*, LVIII, 3, Summer, 1950). This is a valuable and stimulating essay. The second quotation is taken from Leone Vivante, *English Poetry and its Contribution to the Knowledge of a Creative Principle*, p. 29.

[14]In Sonnet CXXIV there is an interesting contrast between self-seeking and disinterested love. The first is assimilated to the merely natural world,

> As subject to Time's love or to Time's hate,
> Weeds among weeds, or flowers with flowers gather'd;

the second is described as "builded far from accident"—that is, it is a human achievement. But in the human order what is "built" (we may say, deliberately sought and willingly fostered) has life in it,—

> And ruin'd love, when it is *built* anew,
> Grows fairer than at first, more strong, far greater.   (Sonnet CXIX)

nizes his own humanity, and that of others, as something essentially other than a product of the natural world, who is really open to nature; neither fascinated nor afraid, he can respond creatively to its creativeness, and, paradoxically, find in nature a symbol for all that is natural in the other sense—that is, most truly human. It is, I think, some such perception as this, attained in *King Lear,* that lies behind and validates the elaborate and imaginatively powerful analogy between the human order and the order of nature in *Macbeth.*

III

There is no vague "philosophy of nature" in *Macbeth.* The nature against which the "unnaturalness" of the Macbeth evil is defined and judged is human nature; and essential characteristics of that nature— its capacity for and intimate dependence on relationship—are powerfully evoked throughout the play. In Act III, scene iv, Macbeth, overcome by his vision of Banquo's ghost, glances back to a time when murder was common, to what will later be known as the Hobbesian state of nature.

> Blood hath been shed ere now, i' th' olden time,
> Ere humane statute purg'd the gentle weal;
> Ay, and since too, murthers have been perform'd
> Too terrible for the ear: the time has been,
> That, when the brains were out, the man would die,
> And there an end; but now, they rise again,
> With twenty mortal murthers on their crowns,
> And push us from our stools. This is more strange
> Than such a murther is.   (III. iv. 74-82)

This is a more profound version of the origins of society than is suggested by the notion of contract or expediency. What "purges" the supposed mere multitude and makes it into a "gentle" commonweal is a decree greater than any law in which it may be embodied, for it is what is dictated by the very fact of being human; if you accept your humanity then you can't murder with impunity. Nor is this simply a matter of judicial punishment: the murdered man "rises" again, in you. Killing may be common in wild nature, but it is not natural to man as man; it is a violation of his essential humanity. When Lady Macbeth describes her husband as "too full o' the milk of human kindness"[15] she intends to be disparaging, as Goneril does when she speaks

---

[15]Too full, that is, "to catch the nearest way." Lady Macbeth invariably uses euphemisms for murder—"must be provided for," "this night's great business," "our great quell."

of Albany's "milky gentleness" or calls him a "milk-liver'd man"
(*King Lear*, I. iv. 351; IV. ii. 50). But what the phrase also says is that
human kindness is natural to man as man, and, like his mother's milk,
nourishes his manhood. When Malcolm accuses himself of imaginary
crimes, and in so doing reflects the evil that Macbeth has brought on
Scotland, the climax is,

> Nay, had I power, I should
> Pour the sweet milk of concord into Hell,
> Uproar the universal peace, confound
> All unity in earth.   (IV. iii. 97-100)

"Concord," "peace," "unity"—these are *active* words, signifying not
a mere absence of disagreeables, a mere deliverance from "continual
fear, and danger of violent death,"[16] but the condition of positive
human living. We learn little about a play by making lists of words,
but it is a significant fact that *Macbeth* contains a very large number of
words expressing the varied relations of life (not only "cousin," "children," "servants," "guest," "host,"...but "thanks," "payment," "service," "loyalty," "duties"...), and that these sometimes, as in Act I,
scenes iv and vi, seem to be dwelt on with a special insistence. At the
end of the play, when Macbeth thinks of what he has lost, it is not
"honour, wealth and ease in waning age" (*Lucrece*, l. 142) but

> that which should accompany old age,
> As honour, love, obedience, troops of friends,   (V. iii. 24-25)

An awareness of those "holy cords" which, though they may be severed,
are "too intrince"—too intimately intertwined—"to unloose" (*King
Lear*, II. ii. 75-76), is integral to the imaginative structure of *Macbeth*. That the man who breaks the bonds that tie him to other men,
who "pours the sweet milk of concord into Hell," is at the same time
violating his own nature and thwarting his own deepest needs, is something that the play dwells on with a special insistence.

Now as we have seen in relation to *King Lear* it is only when the
essential needs and characteristics of human nature are given an
absolute, unconditional priority, that nature in its widest sense can be
invoked as an order underlying, invigorating, and in a certain sense
offering a pattern for, human nature. So too in *Macbeth*. In Macbeth's
apocalyptic soliloquy before the murder, the "Pity" that dominates
the chaotic natural forces and rides the whirlwind appears as a new-

---

[16]Hobbes, *Leviathan* (Everyman edition), I, 13, p. 65. "The Passions that encline men
to Peace," says Hobbes, "are Fear of Death; Desire of such things as are necessary to com-
modious living; and a Hope by their Industry to obtain them" (p. 66)—which is true, but
only part of the truth.

born babe—an offspring of humanity, naked, vulnerable, and powerful. It is, we may say, because of the symbol of the babe, and all it
stands for, that Shakespeare can invoke the powers of nature and associate them, as Professor Wilson Knight shows that he does, with all that
is opposed to, and finally victorious over, the powers of destruction.[17]
It is in the scene of Duncan's entry into Macbeth's castle (I. vi.)—
"a perfect contrast in microcosm to the Macbeth evil"[18]—that we are
most vividly aware of the energies of untaught nature in significant
relation to the human order. The scene is set for full dramatic effect
between Lady Macbeth's invocation of the powers of darkness ("The
raven himself is hoarse,/ That croaks the fatal entrance...") and Macbeth's final resolution, and Duncan's courtesy underlines the irony.
But the contrast is not confined to the situation. The suggestion of a
sweet fresh air, the pleased contemplation of the birds that build and
breed, affect us first as sensory contrasts to the smothering oppression
("Come, thick Night...") so recently evoked; but like the images of
darkness and disorder the presented scene is inseparable from the
values it embodies and defines.

> This guest of summer,
> The temple-haunting martlet, does approve,
> By his lov'd mansionry, that the heaven's breath
> Smells wooingly here: no jutty, frieze,
> Buttress, nor coign of vantage, but this bird
> Hath made his pendent bed, and procreant cradle:
> Where they most breed and haunt, I have observ'd
> The air is delicate.

What we are contemplating here is a natural and wholesome *order,*
of which the equivalent in the human sphere is to be found in those
mutualities of loyalty, trust and liking that Macbeth proposes to
violate. And it is an order that is at one with the life it fosters. The

---

[17]See "The Milk of Concord: an Essay on Life Themes in *Macbeth,*" in *The Imperial
Theme,* especially pp. 140-41, 144-45, 148-51. In contrast, Macbeth projects onto Nature
his own malice; for example at III, ii, 13-15—

> We have scorch'd the snake, not kill'd it;
> She'll close, and be herself; whilst our poor malice
> Remains in danger of her former tooth.

We do not need to ask ourselves what the snake is that will "close." Macbeth is dimly
aware of a hostile world with which he is committed to an unending struggle.

[18]*The Imperial Theme,* p. 142. F. R. Leavis, in "How to Teach Reading" (*Education
and the University,* pp. 122-24) gives a characteristically sure and sensitive account of
the imaginative effect of the first ten lines of this scene.

opening lines of the scene, in short, are not only beautiful in them-selves, they form an image of life delighting in life. It is in terms of destructive and self-destructive energies that Macbeth's power lust is defined; and it is from the "life" images of the play, which range from the temple-haunting martlets to Macduff's "babes," his "pretty ones," and include all the scattered references to man's natural goods —sleep and food and fellowship—that we take our bearings in the ap-prehension of evil.

IV

In the great soliloquy of I. vii. Macbeth tries to provide himself with prudential reasons for not committing murder: —

> But in these cases,
> We still have judgment here; that we but teach
> Bloody instructions, which, being taught, return
> To plague th'inventor.

But the attempt at a cool calculation of consequences (already at odds with the nervous rhythm and the taut muscular force of the imagery of the opening lines) almost immediately gives way to an appalling vision of judgment.

> Besides, this Duncan
> Hath borne his faculties so meek, hath been
> So clear in his great office, that his virtues
> Will plead like angels, trumpet-tongu'd, against
> The deep damnation of his taking-off....

These lines have of course behind them the traditional conception of the Day of Judgment, and it is nothing less than the nature of judg-ment that the play reveals. Just as, in Spinoza's words "blessedness is not the reward of virtue but virtue itself," so the deep damnation of this play is revealed in the intrinsic qualities of an evil deliberately willed and persisted in. It is revealed above all as a defection from life and reality.

> So that in vent'ring ill we leave to be
> The things we are for that which we expect;
> And this ambitious foul infirmity,
> In having much, torments us with defect
> Of that we have: so then we do neglect

> The things we have, and, all for want of wit,
> Make something nothing by augmenting it.

So Shakespeare had written in *The Rape of Lucrece* (ll. 148-154), where lust—a type of sin, "including all foul harms" (l. 199)—was defined as the urge to possess something that in the experience inevitably proves mere loss, an over-reaching into insubstantiality and negation.[19] In *Macbeth* the positives so securely established—the assured intimation of "the things we [*sc.* truly] are"—throw into relief, and so sharply define, the defection that occupies the forefront of the play. It is this that makes the play's irony so deeply significant—the irony of making "something nothing by augmenting it," that is, in Banquo's phrase, "by seeking to augment it" (II. i. 27); and that central irony of losing in gaining—for Macbeth, like Tarquin, is "A captive victor that hath lost in gain" (*Lucrece,* l. 730)—lies behind all the often noted dramatic ironies that multiply as the play proceeds. Fear and disorder erupt into the specious security and apparent order that temporarily succeed the murder of Duncan.[20] "Things bad begun" attempt to "make strong themselves by ill," yet each further step is as "tedious" (Macbeth's word) and self-frustrating as the last. And the concomitant of the outer disorder and inner disintegration (with both of which Macbeth identifies himself in the great invocation of chaos in IV. i.) is something that appears to the observer as the betrayal of life to automatism, and within Macbeth's own consciousness as a deepening sense of the loss of significance. It is a radical failure of the human to inhabit his proper world of creative activity. A brief examination of these two related aspects of that failure will conclude our examination of the play's philosophy.

We touch for the last time on the question of "nature." Early in the play we are told of "the merciless Macdonwald" that he is "worthy to be a rebel,"

---

[19]Parallels between *Macbeth* and *Lucrece* are noted by Professor Kenneth Muir in Appendix C of his Arden edition of the play. Of "defect" in the lines quoted above, where a slight immaturity of style cannot conceal the maturity of the thought, C. Knox Pooler, in a note in the Arden edition, says, "Probably…'the absence of what is really present' rather than 'something lacking to our possessions'."

[20]This is symbolized by the banquet scene (III. iv) where the formal ceremony of the opening ("You know your own degrees, sit down: at first/ And last, the hearty welcome") contrasts with the "admir'd disorder" of the close. Macbeth's inner chaos—"confusion," now, having "made its masterpiece"—is similarly reflected later in the uncoordinated violence of his "royal preparation" for the battle, on which the Doctor dryly comments (V. iii. 57-58). "Sin is an act of violence in itself," says Benjamin Whichcote; "the sinner doth force himself, and stirs up strife within himself."—F. J. Powicke, *The Cambridge Platonists,* pp. 75-76.

> for to that
> The multiplying villainies of nature
> Do swarm upon him.   (I. ii. 9-12)

Now nature, we have seen, is a power that can be invoked in the service of what is essentially right and wholesome on the sole condition that "human kindness" is recognized as an absolute. Nature by itself, however, is clearly a submoral world,[21] and to "Night's black agents" (III. ii. 53) in the outer world correspond, within,

> the cursed thoughts that nature
> Gives way to in repose.   (II. i. 8-9)

Man, the inhabitant of two worlds, is free to choose; but if, disregarding the "compunctious visitings of Nature," he chooses "Nature's mischief" (I. v. 45, 50), his freedom is impaired. He has "untied the winds" (IV. i. 52), and the powers of nature enter the human sphere as autonomous agents: in the language of the play, the "villainies of nature" "swarm upon him" as a more or less passive host.[22]

The explanation of this phrase thus involves us in a consideration of one of the main structural lines of the play, where to the creative energy of good—enlisting and controlling nature's powers—is opposed the automatism of evil. To listen to the witches, it is suggested, is like eating "the insane root,/ That takes the reason prisoner" (I. iii. 84-85); for Macbeth, in the moment of temptation, "function," or intellectual activity, is "smother'd in surmise"; and everywhere the imagery of darkness suggests not only the absence or withdrawal of light but— "light thickens"—the presence of something positively oppressive and impeding. Both Macbeth and his wife wilfully blind themselves ("Come, thick Night," "Come, seeling Night..."), and to the extent that they surrender the characteristically human power of intellectual and moral discernment they themselves become the "prey" of "Night's black agents," of the powers they have deliberately invoked.[23] Automatism is perhaps most obvious in Lady Macbeth's sleep-walking, with its obsessed reliving of the past, but Macbeth also is shown as

---

[21]Savage nature is not insisted on as it is in *King Lear,* but the repeated references to birds of prey and to those members of the animal kingdom for which men tend to feel some instinctive dread or repugnance—shark, tiger, wolf, etc.—do not allow us to forget that aspect of the play's background.

[22]So too "boundless intemperance" is "a tyranny" (IV. iii. 66-67).

[23]Two articles by L. A. Cormican on "Medieval Idiom in Shakespeare" (*Scrutiny*, XVII, 3 and 4) contain many pregnant reflections on the relation of moral to psychological insights in this play and in Shakespeare generally, and on the relation of both to the prevailing tradition.

forfeiting his human freedom and spontaneity. If one ultimate aspect
of evil is revealed in Macbeth's invocation of chaos, in his determina-
tion to be answered,

> though the treasure
> Of Nature's germens tumble all together,
> Even till destruction sicken,

another is suggested by the banal repetitions of the witches' incantations, the almost mechanical beat in which their charms are "wound
up." And just as the widespreading confusion (enacted on the "metaphysical" plane) is reflected in the particular action, so Macbeth's
terror-stricken advance in evil is tuned to that monotonous beat. "One
feels," says W. C. Curry, "that in proportion as the good in him dimin-
ishes, his liberty of free choice is determined more and more by evil
inclination and that he cannot choose the better course. Hence we
speak of destiny or fate, as if it were some external force or moral
order, compelling him against his will to certain destruction."[24]
Most readers have felt that after the initial crime there is something
compulsive in Macbeth's murders; and at the end, for all his "valiant
fury," he is certainly not a free agent. He is like a bear tied to a stake,
he says; but it is not only the besieging army that hems him in; he is
imprisoned in the world he has made.

It is from within that world that, prompted by the news of his wife's
suicide, he speaks his last great speech.

> She should have died hereafter:
> There would have been a time for such a word.
> To-morrow, and to-morrow, and to-morrow,
> Creeps in this petty pace from day to day,
> To the last syllable of recorded time;
> And all our yesterdays have lighted fools
> The way to dusty death. Out, out, brief candle!
> Life's but a walking shadow; a poor player,
> That struts and frets his hour upon the stage,
> And then is heard no more: it is a tale
> Told by an idiot, full of sound and fury,
> Signifying nothing.   (V. v. 17-28)

His wife's death, it has often been observed, means nothing to him.
Commentators have been exercised to determine the precise meaning
of the words with which he greets it—"She should have died here-

[24]Walter Clyde Curry, *Shakespeare's Philosophical Patterns*, p. 105. [See also this
volume pp. 30-33.]

after" ("She would have died sometime," or, "Her death should have been deferred to a more peaceable hour"); but the point of the line lies in its ambiguity. Macbeth is groping for meanings, trying to conceive a time when he might have met such a situation with something more than indifference, when death itself might have had a significance it cannot have in the world of mere meaningless repetition that he goes on to evoke.[25] As a final irony this *is* the world where when a thing is done it is merely—"alms for oblivion"—done with, because it is a world devoid of significant relations.

Clearly then we have in this play an answer to Shakespeare's earlier questionings about time's power, as we have also a resolution of his earlier preoccupation with the power of illusion and false appearance. Macbeth *has betrayed himself* to the equivocal and the illusory. So too time appears to him as meaningless repetition because he has turned his back on, has indeed attempted violence on, those values that alone give significance to duration, that in a certain sense make time, for "Without the meaning there is no time."[26] He has directed his will to evil, towards something that of its very nature makes for chaos and the abnegation of meaning. The solid natural goods— ranging from food and sleep to the varied mutualities of friendship, service, love—are witnesses to the central paradox of evil, that however terrible its power it can only lead to "nothing."

In the lines,

> ...it is a tale
> Told by an idiot, full of sound and fury,
> Signifying nothing,

there is combined the apparent force—the sound and fury—and the essential meaninglessness. For Macbeth, now, though in a different sense from when he used the phrase, "nothing is, but what is not."[27]

But the play's last word is not, of course, about evil.

---

[25]Middleton Murry, in a chapter of his *Shakespeare* significantly called "The Time Has Been," catches the sinister significance of the dubious phrase, but I cannot properly understand the conclusion to which he proceeds. [See this volume pp. 22-29.]

[26]T. S. Eliot, *The Rock*.

[27]"No evil passion pursued to the end," says Berdyaev, "has any positive content. All evil consumes itself. Its nothingness is laid bare by its own inner course of development. Evil is the sphere of phantasy (an idea admirably developed by St. Athanasius the Great). Evil is evil not because it is forbidden but because it is non-being."—*Freedom and the Spirit*, p. 183. The same idea is expressed in the *Revelations of Divine Love*, by Julian of Norwich: see especially Chapters XI ("Sin is no deed"), XXVII, and LXIII. The traditional doctrine of the essentially negative quality of evil, with especial reference to *Macbeth*, is admirably described by Walter Clyde Curry in *Shakespeare's Philosophical Patterns*.

>   What's more to do,
> Which would be planted newly with the time—
> As calling home our exil'd friends abroad,
> That fled the snares of watchful tyranny;
> Producing forth the cruel ministers
> Of this dead butcher, and his fiend-like Queen,
> Who, as 'tis thought, by self and violent hands
> Took off her life—this, and what needful else
> That calls upon us, by the grace of Grace,
> We will perform in measure, time, and place.

It is a fitting close for a play in which moral law has been made present to us not as convention or command but as the law of life itself, as that which makes for life, and through which alone man can ground himself on, and therefore in his measure know, reality.

The Story of the Night: *Macbeth*

by John Holloway

There is a clear sense, in *Hamlet* and to a lesser extent in *Othello*, that a retributive justice works through human life, and that an order and symmetry may therefore be seen in the doings of men. In *Macbeth* this is more conspicuous still. First, it is a substantial part of the whole movement of the action. Moreover, the action itself is seen in a perspective which extends beyond the doings of men, since it takes in the environment of Nature within which these doings occur, and from which in the end they seem to derive their quality. *Macbeth,* that is to say, is a work which offers the spectator no view of life alone, but a view of life which is part of a view of the world. In a broad and perhaps old-fashioned sense of the term, it is a philosophical play as *Hamlet* and *Othello* are not.

What opens up this wider perspective of life is nothing short of the play's total dynamic; but this includes far more than any mere "what happens to the characters" seen in simple terms. The characters, taken in themselves, have to thread their way through an ampler body of experience proffered to the spectator; and for him, this ampler body of experience, this poetic richness of the play, is less conspicuous as chains of imagery which he could list as mere words in his study, than as images in the true sense, images which seem to people the stage, which have an independent life in the experience before him. It is in this sense, a sense which takes us beyond "language" considered by itself, that *Macbeth* is a more than realistic, a truly poetic play.

At the opening of *Macbeth,* Macbeth himself is the centre of respect and interest. He is the cynosure, the present saviour of the state.

> ...brave Macbeth — well he deserves that name —
> Disdaining Fortune, with his brandish'd steel
> Which smoked with bloody execution,
> Like *valour's minion,* carv'd out his passage.... (I. ii. 16)

With these vivid words, the absent is present: the minion of valour and disdainer of Fortune is sharply before our imagination in all the slaughter of civil war. Yet this image of Macbeth is ambivalent. Only a few lines before, in the explosive opening words of the very first scene (other than that of the witches, no clear part of human life at all), Shakespeare has provided his audience, before their eyes and on stage, with an actual picture that the account of Macbeth in battle, quoted just now, disquietingly resembles:

> What bloody man is that? He can report,
> As seemeth by his plight, of the *revolt*
> The newest state.   (I. ii. 1)

But insofar as we identify Macbeth with the image of a man stained in blood, and his weapon dripping with blood, he is no image merely of a destroyer of revolt. By a more direct and primitive mode of thought, by simple association, he is an image of revolt itself. The doubtful goodness of his disdaining Fortune (of which more must be said later) appears in a new, uneasy light.

This image of the bloody man is so much insisted on in the opening scenes, that it is not enough to call it an image. It is an apparition. It haunts the stage. Ross says that Macbeth was:

> Not afraid of what thyself didst make,
> Strange *images of death*.   (I. iii. 96)

Again, the ambiguous phrasing carries weight. It is the same hideous sight which is the "horrid image" seen by Macbeth, in imagination, after his meeting with the witches (I. iii. 135); and that we see, in Macbeth himself, when he enters after the murder of Duncan, and invites our contemplation almost as if he were an emblem of violence ("this is a sorry sight," II. ii. 20). Again, it is the same image that we must call to mind when Macbeth says that he will not return to see the spectacle of the murdered Duncan (II. ii. 50); and that Lady Macbeth says she will make the grooms look like; and that Lennox revives once more for us in his account of the grooms ("their hands and faces were all badged with blood" (II. iii. 100). It is "the great doom's image" that Macbeth himself sees in Duncan lying dead when he tells the lords of the murder (II. iii. 60). This image, kept so much before our imagination that it seems without exaggeration to stalk the stage, is the image with which Macbeth is identified in the very first account we have of him. From the start, he may be valour's minion, but he impresses our minds as the bloody man, the image of death.

The apparition was not coined by Shakespeare. Its force is greater and its meaning clearer than that, for it is a traditional image from the Bible. "Come foorth thou bloodshedder" ("man of blood" is the gloss: II Sam., 16.7); or again, "the Lord wyll abhorre the bloodthirstie and deceitful man" (Ps. 5, 6). Macbeth himself makes the exact verbal connection: he speaks (III. v. 126) of how augurs have "brought forth/ The secret'st *man of blood.*" We must therefore go much further than to say, with Professor Knights, that in the early part of the play the "theme" of "the reversal of values" is prominently "stated."[1] The play opens with something not static and discursive, but violent, integral to the play, and dynamic: an "image of revolt," the image of an actual *deed* of overturning, which serves from the start as emblem both of the central character, and of the course of the action.

The double nature of Macbeth is emphasized by a turn of events at the beginning of the play which would be distracting and confusing if it did not serve exactly this purpose. This is the introduction of the Norwegian invaders, who upset Macbeth's victory over the rebel Macdonwald by their inopportune arrival. By itself, this would be wholly distracting. It is only not so, through the significance which is given to it. The new threat of danger to the state is made to underline the conflicting meanings in Macbeth's victory over the rebels. "From that spring, whence comfort seem'd to come/ Discomfort swells," says the Sergeant (I. ii. 25): comparing the event with the coming of clouds that obscure the sun, and bring at first welcome shade, but then un-welcome storm. Both the comparison with the sun (ruler of the sky as the king is of the country), and the Sergeant's later assertion that Macbeth (and also Banquo) respond to the new challenge as if they meant to bring about "another Golgotha" (l. 41) reinforce the effect. The Norweigians, soon forgotten, free Shakespeare to suggest, even before there is any imputation against Macbeth, that his deliverance of the state is also the opposite of a deliverance.

The nature of Macbeth's conduct, and the experience for ourselves which this makes of the play, are quite misunderstood if he is thought, however, to be an "image of revolt" merely at the level of civil dis-obedience. The significance of what he does goes deeper. It must any-how do this, if only by implication. That rebellion against the lawful king counted as rebellion against God was a commonplace of the time. The idea may be illustrated by many quotations from obvious sources such as the *Mirror for Magistrates* or the Elizabethan *Homilies;* and it simply follows, from that essential correspondence between the

[1]*Explorations* (1946), p. 18.

order of civil government and the order of nature, which (as everyone knows by now) was one of the basic ideas of Shakespeare's time, and appeared repeatedly in his work. Yet for *Macbeth*, to see this is not to see enough. It is not merely by implication that Macbeth's act of revolt is more than civic, is an ultimate revolt. It is this, clearly and with emphasis, from the start. At its inception, his plot makes his heart knock against his ribs "against the use of nature" (I. iv. 137); Duncan on his death-bed looks "like a breach in Nature/ For Ruin's wasteful entrance" (a rich line, in which the image of Duncan himself, as bloody man, is transformed into the image of the revolt of which he is victim, and the ruin which must prove its sequel). After Banquo's ghost disrupts the feast, Macbeth thinks of how "the secret'st man of blood" has been given away:

> Stones have been known to move, and trees to speak;
> (III. v. 123)

But the line seems to call up miracles in the past less than it suggests the anti-nature which Macbeth has created, not only in his own mind, in the present. The sense of Macbeth's career as one of revolt against everything in the world is even sustained by lines like those of Ross describing the woes of Scotland:

> good men's lives
> Expire before the flowers in their caps.
> Dying or ere they sicken.
> (IV. iii. 171)

This is no vivid Shakespearean innovation: and to find that men are seen in it as among all the earth's other living things is merely to hear its echoes in tradition:

> Thou turnest man to destruction…they…fade away sodainly lyke the grasse. In the morning it is green & groweth up: but in the evenyng it is cut downe, dryed up, and wythered.   (Ps. 90)

Again, it is no fact of disorder we are offered, but an act; one of giant divergence whose rise and fall preoccupies the spectator from the "innocent flower" which Lady Macbeth tells her husband to seem like at the outset (I, v, 62), to the "sere and yellow leaf" into which he finds that his way (or May?) of life has fallen in the autumn of his career. His anti-Nature has had its year, like Nature itself.

The word "disorder" offers no more than a vague blur in the direction of what this anti-Nature essentially is. From the very opening of the play, when the witches plan "to meet with Macbeth" (I, i, 8), we have a clear clue, which may be brought into focus by reference to Burton's catalogue of the kinds of evil spirits:

> ...the fifth kind are cozeners, such as belong to magicians *and witches: their prince is Satan*[2]

One after the other, and with much greater deliberateness than Othello, Lady Macbeth and then Macbeth dedicate themselves formally to evil, and more specifically, to the powers of evil in traditional terms:

> Come, you spirits
> That tend on mortal thoughts, unsex me here...
> That no compunctious visitings of nature
> Shake my fell purpose....   (I. v. 37)

The formalized moment of self-dedication shows as clearly here as it does in Macbeth's own prayer later:

> Now o'er the one half-world
> Nature seems dead...
>   ...thou sure and firm-set Earth,
> Hear not my steps....   (II. i. 49)

But that we are to see it as dedication to the Satanic itself is reserved for a later moment, that of Macbeth's resolution to murder Banquo:

> Come seeling Night...
> And with thy bloody and invisible hand
> Cancel and tear to pieces that great bond
> Which keeps me pale...
>   (III. ii. 46)

"bloody hand" and "tear to pieces" resurrect, behind the words "which keeps me pale," the recurrent apparition of the play: Macbeth's prayer is to be transformed, once for all, into the man of blood. By whose power this is to be done, is made clear in the lines which follow almost immediately:

> Good things of day begin to droop and drowse,
> While night's black agents to their preys do rouse.

In the last episode of the play, the combat between Macbeth and Macduff, it is made plain that night's black agents are the fallen angels, the powers of Satan himself:

[2]*Anatomy of Melancholy,* 1.2.1.2.

> Despair thy charm;
> And let the *angel* which thou still hast served
> Tell thee Macduff was from his mother's womb
> Untimely ripped.   (V. viii. 33)

—and also that at the end Macbeth admits, and defiantly faces, the known reward of such service:

> lay on, Macduff;
> And *damn'd* be him that first cries "Hold, enough!"

That the rôle of the Macbeths is one of service to the principle of evil itself has one consequence which is especially important, because it recurs:

> Though you untie the winds and let them fight
> Against the churches; though the yesty waves
> Confound and swallow navigation up;
> Though bladed corn be lodg'd [flattened] and trees blown down;
> Though castles topple on their warders' heads;
> Though palaces and pyramids do slope
> Their heads to their foundations; though the treasure
> Of nature's germens tumble all together,
> Even till destruction sicken—answer me
> To what I ask you.   (IV. i. 52)

In these words Macbeth "conjures" the witches (it is again, as that word suggests, a formalized speech, a recognizable and ritual act), to tell him what he needs to know, even at the cost of universal destruction. In effect, the lines come near to a curse upon the whole of Nature. Rebellion has been taken to its full extent.

There is another "apparition" (as it might be called) besides that of the bloody man, which haunts this play, and expresses and symbolizes this aspect of Macbeth's role, his journey in the direction of universal chaos. It is that of riders and horses, and it seems to have gone unnoticed by critics up to now. To register the full contribution which this image makes to the play, one should call to mind something of what the armed rider, and indeed the horse itself (that almost extinct animal, at least in the *milieu* of critics) stood for in Shakespeare's society, as for millennia before. The armed rider was the surest and swiftest of all human messengers, and the signal embodiment of violence, warfare, brigandage, revolt. The horse was the most powerful and valuable of the species which served man, and at the same time, if it rebelled, the most spirited, mischievous and formidable.

Both were deeply ambiguous figures, inviting admiration and fear at once.

How these images contribute to *Macbeth* becomes clearer, in fact, once their contribution to *Lear* is seen as well; but even without anticipating this feature of that play, the facts are plain enough. The oft-quoted horses of Duncan that "turned wild in nature" and ate each other like monsters (II, iv, 14) should be seen in this light: their monstrous act is the more terrifying because it brings to life what within the world of the play is a permanently latent fear. A passage from the *Homily against Wilful Rebellion* illuminates this episode. When married men revolt, it runs, they leave their wives at home, which is bad enough. It is much worse when the unmarried revolt: "being now by rebellion set at liberty from correction of laws, they pursue other men's wives and daughters...*worse than any stallions or horses.*"[3] Unexpectedly perhaps for our own time, it is the horse which proves to be the obvious illustration of unbridled violence. The disturbing image runs throughout the play. The crucial scenes of the murder in Macbeth's castle at Inverness are set in the context of the arrival first of the Macbeth's messenger:

> One of my fellows had the speed of him,
> Who, almost dead for breath, had scarcely more
> Than would make up his message.   (I. v. 32)

and then of the furiously galloping Macbeth himself:

> *Duncan.* Where's the Thane of Cawdor?
> We coursed him at the heels and had a purpose
> To be his purveyor; but he rides well,
> And his great love, sharp as his spur, hath holp him
> To his home before us.   (I. iv. 20)

The murderers waiting for Banquo and Fleance hear their horses' hooves as they stand waiting in the dark. "Hark, I hear horses," says the Third Murderer (III, iii, 8): and Macbeth's earlier "I wish your horses sure and swift of foot" (III, i, 37) has made it clear that the horses (in imagination, or by theatrical device) are at a gallop. We are to envisage the same before Macbeth's last battle:

> Send out more horses, skirr the country round,
> Hang those that talk of fear   (V. iii. 35)

[3]Homily *Against Disobedience and Wilful Rebellion,* the Third Part (Homilies, 1859 ed., p. 574).

and it is this sound again which Macbeth hears after his last meeting with the witches:

> Infected be the air whereon they ride;
> And damn'd all those that trust them! I did hear
> The galloping of horse. Who was't came by?   (IV. i. 138)

What he hears, moreover (or so the spectator's impression should run), is not the presumably soundless riding away of the witches, nor merely that of the men who bring him news of Macduff's flight to England. In the last analysis, he hears also those who properly preside unseen at such a meeting; and these are the

> heaven's cherubim hors'd
> Upon the sightless couriers of the air

of his first soliloquy (I, vii, 22). Nor is the word "hors'd" here wholly figurative: a more literal interpretation of it will bring to mind heavenly cherubim that belong to this context, and that come down from a then universally known passage of scripture:

> And I sawe, and beholde, a white horse, and hee that sate on hym had a bowe, and a crowne was geuen ynto hym, and he went foorth conquering, and for to overcome....And there went out another horse that was redde: and power was geuen to him that sate thereon to take peace from the earth, and that they should kyl one another....And I beholde, and loe, a blacke horse: and he that sate on hym hadde a pair of ballances in his hand....And I looked, and beholde a pale horse, & his name that sate on hym was death, and hel folowed with him: and power was geuen vnto them, ouer the fourth part of the earth, to kyl with sworde, & with hunger, and with dearth, and with the beastes of the earth.   (Rev. 6, 2-8)

The horses that Macbeth hears galloping are the Four Horsemen of the Apocalypse: bringing, as they ride over the earth, the disasters which are the proper result of, proper retribution for, human evil.

   That the play depicts disorder spreading throughout a whole society ("bleed, bleed poor country": IV, iii, 32) is a commonplace. So is it, indeed, that this is seen as an infringement of the whole beneficent order of Nature; and that nothing less than that whole beneficent order gears itself, at last, to ending the state of evil ("...the pow'rs above/ Put on their instruments," IV, iii, 238). That the coming of Birnam Wood to Dunsinane is a vivid emblem of this, a dumbshow of nature overturning anti-nature at the climax of the play, has gone unnoticed. Professor Knights once suggested that in this scene, "nature becomes unnatural in order to rid itself of Macbeth," or rather, that it was "emphasizing the disorder" by showing the forces of good in association with deceit and with the *un*natural.[4] To a contemporary audience, however, the scene must have presented a much more familiar and less unnatural appearance than it does to ourselves. The single figure, dressed in his distinctive costume (one should have Macbeth in his war equipment in mind) pursued by a whole company of others carrying green branches, was a familiar sight as a Maying procession, celebrating the triumph of new life over the sere and yellow leaf of winter. Herrick's *Corinna's Going a-Maying* brings out not only the gaiety of the occasion, and its intimate connections with procreation and new life even in the human sphere, but also how familiar such scenes must have been in Shakespeare's time and indeed long after:

> There's not a budding youth, or girl, this day
> But is got up, and gone to bring in May.
>   A deal of youth, ere this, is come
>   Back, and with white-thorn laden home.
> And some have wept, and wooed, and plighted troth,
>   Many a green-gown has been given
>   Many a kiss both odd and even...
> Many a jest told of the keys betraying
> This night, and locks picked, yet we're not a-Maying.

One should remember that the May procession, with its green branches, survived even in the London Strand until as late as the 1890s.

To a certain extent, Macbeth's career through the play almost invites being seen against the patterns of this primitive kind of ritual. Like any Lord of Misrule, he has (at least in metaphor) his ill-fitting, borrowed robes:

> now does he feel his title
> Hang loose about him, like a giant's robe
> Upon a dwarfish thief.   (V. ii. 20)

Moreover, he has his Feast (III. iv.) that proves only the mockery of a feast. But the interest of these details is increased, if we call to mind that there are certain features of Macbeth's career which not only fall obviously into place here, but also closely resemble moments which have already been distinguished in *Hamlet* and *Othello*. Macbeth's transition from Lord of Misrule and image of revolt to victim of the abiding and restorative forces of life is one, in fact, with that progres-

---

[4]*Explorations*, p. 34.

sive isolation which (like Hamlet and Othello) he clearly undergoes.
The sons of Duncan flee him, Fleance flees, Macduff

> denies his person
> At our great bidding...   (III. iv. 128)

and his other followers are shams as well:

> There's not a one of them, but in his house
> I keep a servant fee'd.   (III. iv. 131)

In the last Act, Macbeth makes his isolation explicit:

> ...that which should accompany old age,
> As honour, love, obedience, troops of friends,
> I must not look to have.   (V. iii. 24)

It is this scene which closes with the Doctor's profession that he too
would desert if he could; and the last episode before the death of
Macbeth himself is the revelation that many of his army abandoned
him:

> ...We have met with foes
> That strike beside us.   (V. vii. 28)

Nor is our experience of merely a process whereby the protagonist
is isolated. As with Othello, we are invited to recognize, and to dwell
on the fact, that this journey of progressive isolation is one with its
distinctive end. The protagonist, transformed bit by bit from leader
to quarry, must at last stand at bay. Macbeth first registers this phase
of his experience in words which resume how it was integral to it to
enrol as an enemy against Nature:

> If this which he avouches does appear,
> There is *nor flying hence nor tarrying here;*
> I 'gin to be a-weary of the sun,
> *And wish th' estate o' th' world were now undone.*
> Ring the alarum bell. Blow wind, come wrack....   (V. v. 47)

He confirms the coming of the final phase in a passage reminiscent
of Othello's "Here is my butt/ And very sea-mark of my utmost sail":

> They have tied me to a stake; I cannot fly,
> But bear-like I must stand the course....   (V. vii. 1)

Nor does the resemblance end there. Macbeth's course, like Othello's,
has been from man to monster. Montano's "O monstrous act" (*Othello,*

V. ii. 183) has its exact parallel in the later play; and, as in *Othello*, it comes in the closing lines, when the movement is complete, and significance at its plainest:

> *Macduff.* Then yield thee, coward,
>   And live to be the gaze and show o' th' time;
>   We'll have thee, *as our rarer monsters are*,
>   Painted upon a pole, and underwrit,
>   "Here you may see the tyrant."   (V. viii. 26)

Finally, Malcolm in his closing speech makes clear what is at issue in the sweeping away of the dominion of the lonely monster, once he has been brought to bay and destroyed. His first thought is to re-establish the social group in all its harmonious plurality, honouring his immediate followers as earls, and

> ...calling home our exil'd friends abroad.   (V. viii. 66)

Isolation is at once to be replaced by community.

The play also moves forward in another dimension: one more intimate and inward than this of society ridding itself of its own monstrous birth, for it explores Macbeth's growing realization of what he has done. Neither in *Othello* nor in *Macbeth* is there really much question of the protagonist's repenting. In the former play, this is not because of any moral failure on Othello's part, but simply because (though many will be loth to admit it) the crucial questions of right are barely raised. Whether Montano would or should have seen Othello's act as monstrous, even had Desdemona really been confirmed in adultery, is left undiscussed. It is Iago who (in Lodovico's words) is the viper. In calling Othello merely a "rash and most unfortunate man," Lodovico confirms how Othello's error of *fact* is now so much the central reality, that the moral judgement most interesting to many in our own age is passed over. The repentance of Othello is concentrated, like the awareness of all those with him, upon his disastrous folly, and is not repentance in the moral sense at all. It is quite otherwise in *Macbeth*. Here, attention is indeed concentrated on the protagonist as not foolish but fiendish. In him, however, there is one glimpse only of something like repentance in the full sense. It comes in the closing scene of the play, and we should surely admire how Shakespeare held this final movement of Macbeth's mind in reserve, sustaining our interest, insight and sympathy at the very last:

> *Macduff:*   Turn hell-hound, turn.
> *Macbeth: Of all men else I have avoided thee.*

> *But get thee back; my soul is too much charged*
> *With blood of thine already.*   (V. viii. 3)

Of Macbeth's genuinely beginning to turn from the evil he has done, I can find no clear hint but this; and even this falls somewhat short of repentance proper.

On the side of intellectual response, what Macbeth comes to recognize, and even in a limited sense regret, is his own error; but this process of realization goes further, and takes in more, than might be thought. Macbeth's career is an illustration, of course, of the traditional belief, which is expressed in three different places in scripture, that "all they that take the sword, shall perish with the sword" (Matth. 26, 52; cf. Gen. 9, 6, and Rev. 13, 10). The central irony is that what Macbeth saw from the start as a mere difficulty in his way is proved, bit by bit, to be inescapable reality, and foreseeable as such:

> This even-handed justice
> Commends the ingredients of our poison'd chalice
> To our own lips....   (I. vii. 10)

"From that spring whence comfort seem'd to come/ Discomfort swells" proves no truer for Duncan than it does, in turn, for Macbeth. Two prominent speeches set the irony beyond overlooking. The first consists in Macbeth's insincere words at the very moment of success. He is announcing the death of Duncan, and alleging that with this, life has lost all meaning:

> Had I but died an hour before this chance
> I had lived a blessed time: for from this instant
> There's nothing serious in mortality;
> All is but toys: renown and grace is dead,
> The wine of life is drawn, and the mere lees
> Is left this vault to brag of.   (II. iii. 89)

The irony goes further than the fact that, as a moral comment on what Macbeth has just done, this is more than a fitting though empty gesture, because it is the sober truth: what completes that irony is how Macbeth echoes these words, later on, in a speech as sincere as this is insincere:

> *Seyton:* The Queen, my lord, is dead.
> *Macbeth.* She should have died hereafter;
>   There would have been a time for such a word.
>   To-morrow, and to-morrow, and to-morrow,
>   Creeps in this petty pace from day to day

> To the last syllable of recorded time,
> And all our yesterdays have lighted fools
> The way to dusty death. Out, out, brief candle!
> Life's but a walking shadow, a poor player,
> That struts and frets his hour upon the stage,
> And then is heard no more; it is a tale
> Told by an idiot, full of sound and fury,
> Signifying nothing.

Whatever may be the exact relation between the first two lines of this speech and the rest, it is clear that the effect of the queen's death is to bring out finally what he has half seen before, when he says

> I am in blood
> Stepp'd in so far that, should I wade no more,
> Returning were as tedious as go o'er.

It is something which also emerges through the irony of Lady Macbeth's account of the murder:

> This night's great business...
> Which shall to all our nights and days to come
> Give solely sovereign sway and masterdom.   (I. v. 65)

What looked as if it would endow life with the greatest meaningfulness has deprived it, in the end, of all meaning. What seemed like the beginning of everything was in fact the end of that, and beginning of nothing. The queen's death does not convince so much as remind Macbeth that he now knows this. Nor, driven as he has been by both inner forces ("these terrible dreams/ That shake us nightly," III, ii, 18) and outer ("the pow'rs above/ Put on their instruments"), is this a reaction to his personal situation alone. His cynicism is general; it is not his own life, but Life, which has come to have no meaning.

Yet this, perhaps, falls short of the exact truth; and it perhaps omits what is vital to the play as a whole. After all, what "all our yesterdays" lighted were "fools"; and what they were lighted to was "dusty death"; and because of the moment when this is said, and the fact that life is seen as one who "struts and frets his hour," as a tale "full of sound and fury," it is impossible not to see this speech as going beyond a vision of total chaos, to a glimpse, or at least an ironical hint, of retributive order. The fools lit to dusty death are less the innocent simpletons, than men like Macbeth himself. His own thought has already pushed out in this direction. The invocation to the witches was prepared to see "nature's germens tumble all together/ *Even till Destruction sicken*"(the passage is quoted in full on p. 112 above). Here too Macbeth knows, or half-knows, what is fatal to his cause. That destruction should indeed sicken is a conviction upon which the whole movement of the play is based. When Fortune "show'd like a rebel's whore," it was glimpsed incompletely. Macbeth "disdained" her too soon; just as Lady Macbeth spoke too easily of "Fate" having crowned her husband (I, v, 26), and Macbeth himself spoke too easily, in inviting Fate to "come into the list" on his side (III, i, 70) against Banquo.

Fate, properly understood, is another kind of thing. To see either it, or Fortune, in these ways, is like seeing only the exposed part of the iceberg. It is the injustice of Fate and Fortune which is even-handed; their justice may come more slowly, but in the end it redresses the balance. And if Macbeth never comes to repent of his actions, he comes at least to comprehend not merely that they brought him no good, but that he could have known this, that he was wrong on a matter of fact, from the start:

> And be these juggling fiends no more believed,
> That palter with us in a double sense,
> That keep the word of promise to our ear
> And break it to our hope.

These are his last words before his final act of animal-like defiance. The fiends are what Burton said: cozeners; and it is a substantial part, not only of Macbeth's response to his ordeal, but also, and still more, of the play's whole action, that fiends are cozeners because Fortune, or Fate, have both this surface meaning, and their true and deeper one.

A passage from Browne's *Religio Medici* makes clear that, once again, Shakespeare has ordered his action upon a belief basic but familiar in his time. Saying that Nature is in effect the Art of God, Browne writes:

> ...this is the ordinary and open way of his Providence...whose effects we may foretel without an Oracle...(but) there is another way...whereof the devil and Spirits have no exact Ephemerides [i.e., calculating tables] ; and that is a more particular and obscure method of his Providence, directing the operations of individuals and single essences: this we call *Fortune,* that serpentine and crooked line, whereby he draws those actions his Wisdom intends, in a more unknown and secret way ...surely there are in every man's Life certain rubs, doublings, and wrenches, which pass a while under the effects of chance, but at the last, well examined, prove the meer hand of God...the lives, not only of men, but of Commonwealths, and the whole World, run not upon an Helix that still enlargeth, but on a Circle, where, arriving to their Meridian, they decline in obscurity, and fall under the Horizon again.

These must not therefore be named the effects of Fortune, but in a relative way, and as we term the works of Nature. It was the ignorance of man's reason that begat this very name, and by a careless term miscalled the Providence of God: for there is no liberty for causes to operate in a loose and stragling way.[5]

Thus *Macbeth* does not start, as does *Othello,* with something like a plain representation of real life. Its opening scenes are dominated less by the human figures in them, than by emblematic images which embody great and indeed terrible forces running through human life, but which appear before us in detachment from the realistically presented characters. Out of a world dominated by these two images, the powers of evil in the witches, and the emblem of revolt in the man of blood, one of the human characters emerges into prominence. At first, this is a prominence which belongs properly to the chief of the king's lieutenants and the saviour of the state.

Yet even from the start, Macbeth is more than, as it were, a plain historical figure. Through his identification with the image of revolt he becomes an icon of one of the great evil potentialities of life. Then, as it is made progressively clearer that his deed of revolt is a deliberate defiance of the whole work of Nature, and a conscious enlistment under the powers of evil, he becomes identified also with the second of these images, the "hell-hound" of Act V scene vii: a plainer and more active embodiment of the satanic power than the witches themselves. Macbeth's status as emblem and embodiment of evil is stressed by his formal self-dedication to this as a way of life (Lady Macbeth pursues the same course), and by his ritualized invocation of universal disaster on Nature in pursuit of his own ends. His actions replace the "bounteous nature" of the kingdom under Duncan by a condition of life which, on the level of explicit political affairs, is one of tyranny, fear, spying and continual murder; and at the level of poetic suggestion is one where ordinary life is haunted — no less emphatic word will serve — haunted by the emblematical images of the evil things of night, the armed rider, the violent horses, the Horsemen, even, of the Apocalypse. These spread through the ordinary patterns of life and give it a new quality of unnatural disruption, strangeness and violence.

As the powers of good re-assert themselves, our perspective is shifted once more. We are now invited to see Macbeth's progress through the contours, as it were, of another image, though one again which has had a long history in human thought and society. We are invited to see him as a kind of ritual victim: a scapegoat, a lord of misrule, who has

[5]Browne, *Religio Medici,* the First Part (*Works,* ed. G. Keynes, 1928, Vol. I, pp. 23-24).

turned life into riot for his limited time, and is then driven out and destroyed by the forces which embody the fertile vitality and the communal happiness of the social group. A vital part of the interest of these closing scenes is Macbeth's own growing consciousness of how what he has done futilely defies these forces, and is sterile and self-destroying.

The element of ritual in the closing scenes, their almost imperceptible relapsing into the contours of a sacrificial fertility ceremony, the expulsion, hunting down and destruction of a man who has turned into a monster, give to the action its final shape. As the action is seen to be turning into this recognizable kind of thing, this activity which has repeatedly been a part of social life, its significance cannot but emerge into final clarity. The suspense and unpredictability which have held the audience's attention so strongly mutate into the working out of a movement which now seems pre-appointed. Macbeth is seen to have strutted and fretted his "hour"; and both this hour, and what bring it to a close, belong to, and represent, one of the basic contours of life. Both depict for us that "particular and obscure method of …Providence" through which the chaos of men's affairs is seen as reposing on an order, and the complexity and entanglement of the play to repose on an underlying form which reflects it.

Macbeth's Disintegration

by A. P. Rossiter

Macbeth, like *Richard III,* is best interpreted through its themes and imagery, not through "character" (contrast *Othello*); and after a consideration of order, kingship and "the state of man" in the Histories. Its unusual shortness (it is the shortest of the tragedies: 2,086 lines, only 70 longer than *The Tempest* and 16 than *A Midsummer Night's Dream)* supports the theory that the Folio (the only text) is a cut version for court-performance. This is consistent with its complimentary allusions to James, his ancestors, his interests. Of the references which establish its date as 1606, that of the Porter to *equivocation* is the most important, because so much of the play turns upon the equivocal: saying both "Ay" and "No" to the "same" thing. This perpetual antithesis is far more than could be inset as a compliment to James for a court-performance. Fr. Henry Garnet was tried on 28 March 1606 for complicity in the Gunpowder Plot, and relied on equivocation to justify his shifty and lying answers. "Tres Sibyllae" greeted James at Oxford, August 1605. There *was* a corn-slump 1605-7; but the farmer "that hang'd himself on th' expectation of plenty" was already a chestnut.

There are really three sources, and of two different sorts:

a. The head and mind of State had been threatened by the powers of evil, who regarded equivocation as justifiable. England and her Scottish King had escaped the chaos of "dire combustion," etc., which would result from blowing up Parliament, from insurrection, from civil war.

b. Holinshed, in his *Chronicles of Scotlande,* has two different stories (of Duff at ii. 149 ff. and of Macbeth at ii. 168-76).

The Gunpowder Plot situation combined in Shakespeare's imagination with the ancient history of James's line; and that with quite another story. Thus Holinshed (p. 171) says that Duncan was a mild and

"Macbeth's Disintegration." From A. P. Rossiter, *Angel with Horns and Other Shakespearean Lectures* (London: Longman Group Ltd., 1961), Chapter II, pp. 209-11. Copyright © 1961 by Longman Group Ltd. Reprinted by permission of the publisher.

incapable king, murdered by Macbeth with Banquo's connivance; and
that Macbeth's wife was "verie ambitious, burning in unquenchable
desire to beare the name of a queene." Macbeth reigned well seven
years, then murdered Banquo, when "every man began to doubt his
own life." Moreover (a detail), "The pricke of conscience…caused
him ever to feare, lest he should be served to the same cup, as he had
ministred to his predecessor" (p. 172). The other Holinshed story is
the murder of King Duff by Donwald for revenge (in a blood-feud),
egged on by his wife, "tho' he abhorred the act greatlie in heart" and
did not do it himself. Duff is entertained as a guest; gives presents;
the Chamberlains are made drunk and killed later by Donwald. Unnatural portents followed for six months (pp. 150-52). Further, Duff
had been troubled by witchcraft at Forres. Holinshed's margin-notes
would recall both stories to any reader who had been over the twenty-
seven pages attentively (though the Siward episode is from his first
volume, *The Chronicles of England,* i. 192).

Shakespeare removed the *external* motive from both murders, i.e.
the *coup d' état* from Duncan's, the blood-feud from Duff's; and
correspondingly increases Duncan's trustfulness, piety, sanctity. The
wilfulness of the murder is thus isolated; and Banquo set contrasting-
ly apart from it.[1]

The outcome is a play about the disintegration of the state of man,
and the state he makes his. It is commonly taken to be "about ambition"; but ambition is only one of the names Macbeth finds for the
impulsion in himself when looking into his own mind:

> I have no spur
> To prick the sides of my intent, but only
> Vaulting ambition, which o'erleaps itself…   (I. vii. 25-27)

and when he names it that, he rejects it: "We will proceed no further.
…" Better, I think, to call it "particular will": a Shakespearian phrase
for a force as much of the "blood" as the intellect: Macbeth's *impulsion*
(rather than his decision, as an ambitious man would feel it) to assert
his pattern on the world: to make Macbeth Scotland. Instead, he finds
he has made Scotland Macbeth: his damned soul has infected a whole
country, even the whole universe. The forces *released* by the hope
held in the Witches' prophecy; by the spurring of his wife, playing on

[1]Over other alleged sources I am sceptical. Professor Kenneth Muir deals well with
them (Introduction to Arden edn., 1951, pp. xl-xli), dismissing, for instance, the pleas of
Mrs. C. C. Stopes and Dr. Dover Wilson that Shakespeare researched in the vast and
deservedly obscure *Buik of the Croniclis of Scotland* by William Stewart.

his soldier's identification of honour (self-hood) with ruthless self-assertion through force: these give him the crown and sceptre. Both are hollow: the "swelling prologue to the imperial theme" leads on to a *shrinking*, till "there's nothing serious in mortality," and he becomes a tortured demon in a hell of his own begetting; glad of his own callousness; and (having half-conquered all), lord of nothing but chaos and the pitifully limited self-assertion of the will to fight until he drops.

General Macbeth

by Mary McCarthy

He is a general and has just won a battle; he enters the scene making a remark about the weather. "So fair and foul a day I have not seen." On this flat note Macbeth's character tone is set. "Terrible weather we're having." "The sun can't seem to make up its mind." "Is it hot/ cold/ wet enough for you?" A commonplace man who talks in commonplaces, a golfer, one might guess, on the Scottish fairways, Macbeth is the only Shakespeare hero who corresponds to a bourgeois type: a murderous Babbitt, let us say....

What is modern and bourgeois in Macbeth's character is his wholly *social* outlook. He has no feeling for others, and yet until the end he is a vicarious creature, existing in his own eyes through others, through what they may say of him, through what they tell him or promise him. This paradox is typical of the social being—at once a wolf out for himself and a sheep. Macbeth, moreover, is an expert buck-passer; he sees how others can be used. It is he, not Lady Macbeth, who thinks of smearing the drunken chamberlains with blood, so that they shall be caught "red-handed" the next morning when Duncan's murder is discovered. At this idea he brightens; suddenly, he sees his way clear. It is the moment when at last he decides. The eternal executive, ready to fix responsibility on a subordinate, has seen the deed finally take a *recognizable* form. Now he can do it. And the crackerjack thought of killing the grooms afterwards (dead men tell no tales—old adage) is again purely his own on-the-spot inspiration; no credit to Lady Macbeth.

It is the sort of thought that would have come to Claudius in *Hamlet,* another trepidant executive. Indeed, Macbeth is more like Claudius than like any other character in Shakespeare. Both are doting husbands; both rose to power by betraying their superior's trust; both are

"General Macbeth." From *Mary McCarthy's Theatre Chronicles 1937-1962* (New York: Farrar, Straus & Giroux, 1963), pp. 235-48. First published in Harper's Magazine, June 1962. Copyright © 1963 by Mary McCarthy. Reprinted by permission of the author.

easily frightened and have difficulty saying their prayers. Macbeth's "Amen" sticks in his throat, he complains, and Claudius, on his knees, sighs that he cannot make what priests call a "good act of contrition." The desire to say his prayers like any pew-holder, quite regardless of his horrible crime, is merely a longing for respectability. Macbeth "repents" killing the grooms, but this is strictly for public consumption. "O, yet I do repent me of my fury, That I did kill them." In fact, it is the one deed he does *not* repent (*i.e.*, doubt the wisdom of) either before or after. This hypocritical self-accusation, which is his sidelong way of announcing the embarrassing fact that he has just done away with the grooms, and his simulated grief at Duncan's murder ("All is but toys; renown and grace is dead; The wine of life is drawn," etc.) are his basest moments in the play, as well as his boldest; here is nearly a magnificent monster.

Macbeth and the Henpecked Hero

by D. J. Enright

Macbeth is a single-minded play, uniquely so among Shakespeare's works, and there would seem to be little for the commentator to say about it at this time; very little indeed, compared with *Lear* and *Antony and Cleopatra*, two plays where the "total situation" involves a more complicated arithmetic. Everybody admires *Macbeth;* nearly everybody has written about it.

And yet, to judge from the recurring confusions into which students fall, some problems still persist. The biggest of these—for if you go wrong here, you go wholly wrong—concerns Macbeth's responsibility or otherwise for the crime he commits, or the degree of responsibility to be attributed to him. Perhaps because their experience of literature runs ahead of their experience of life, students tend to conceive of evil as something large, vague and exciting, which exists outside of human beings, which is indeed too exciting, too momentous, to be at all closely attached to mere men and women, to be relevant to such creatures as their parents and teachers. For some of them the play should not be entitled *Macbeth,* but *Evil* or (in the case of the more pragmatic) *Disorder.*

For others it should be called *The Weird Sisters* or *Lady Macbeth,* since the former are not mere men or women and the latter (since first impressions count for a lot) is more a witch than a wife. Such readers will find G. Wilson Knight's commentary in *The Wheel of Fire* extremely congenial, since he begins with "the inner state of disintegration, disharmony and fear, from which is born an act of crime and destruction," a state of mind to which he refuses to give so mean a name as "ambition." He stresses the notion of "the objectivity of evil": evil "comes from without," and thus it is, he maintains, that "the Weird Sisters are objectively conceived." Evil comes from without— as if it were some species of radioactivity emanating from another planet and unamenable to scientific investigation. The consequence of applying this conception of evil is that Macbeth can only be seen as the innocent victim of an epidemic or a traffic accident or, better, a collision with a meteorite. One would certainly not reproach Professor Wilson Knight with the cold-bloodedness found in some other twentieth-century critics, but here, in the good cause of bringing out the play's momentousness, he has simply reduced its significance. That we cannot praise "the Gods," the supernatural powers, for dealing out unequivocal justice in the play of *Lear* is not sufficient reason for blaming them for the outbreak of unequivocal evil in the play of *Macbeth*. I am setting aside the shaky theory which has it that assent on the part of the spectator to the irresistible potency of the supernatural solicitings will have the advantage of allowing Macbeth to retain, or in some way, usefully seem to retain, a large slice of his "original" nobility of character.

One of the teacher's concerns, then, will be to save Macbeth from shrinking under the influence of metaphysical magic into a poor little man (whose clothes do not fit!), henpecked by his wife, by the Weird Sisters, and by Evil Absolute and Disembodied. Another, however, will be to save him from that reading of the play which leads students to answer the good old question, "Do you consider that Macbeth is an absolute monster?", with a simple though wordy "Yes." It is even possible that Macbeth will have to be defended against both views simultaneously, when he is seen as an absolutely monstrous, henpecked weakling.

Killing the King: *Macbeth*

by Maynard Mack, Jr.

Macbeth ends with a restoration of order that is unmatched in fulness and dramatic weight in the other tragedies. Yet no words can quite describe the hard, somber mood of the end of this play. In simplest terms, what has been shown is that killing the king is *almost* inevitably to be attempted and yet is *almost* inevitably unperformable. The king can be killed, but the whole world, human, natural, and supernatural, reacts to offer a new king. Regicide is finally in some strange way impossible, for better and for worse. At a profounder level, what we have been shown is the destruction of a soul, whose intuitions of a life beyond life are his glory and become his ruin; we go from the savageries within a man to the savageries of the battle that cuts him down, from a hero who sees more deeply into the abyss than we do to a villain who, like his opposers, sees far less. Regicide easily becomes a mysterious sort of suicide, spiritual and physical.[1] It is this ironic distance between us and the protagonist and also between us and the antagonists that lends the somber though reassuring tone to the play's end. In Northrop Frye's terms,[2] *Macbeth* is an autumn tragedy heading toward the winter of irony, whereas *Richard II* and *Hamlet* bestride the middle of the tragic spectrum, equidistant from ironic winter and romantic summer....

[1]This sense of regicide as a form of suicide links the plays I have here considered with *King Lear,* and even, by extension, with *Othello* in ways that need still to be explored. Albert Camus brilliantly summarizes this movement in a passage describing a different king killing and alluding to Brutus, but obviously applicable to Macbeth: "[he] who must kill himself if he does not kill others, begins by killing others. But there are too many; they cannot all be killed. In that case he must die and demonstrate, yet again, that rebellion, when it gets out of hand, swings from the annihilation of others to the destruction of the self." See *The Rebel,* trans. Anthony Bower (New York: Random House, 1956), pp. 128-29.

[2]*Anatomy of Criticism* (Princeton: Princeton University Press, 1957), pp. 158-239.

In *Macbeth,* killing the king reaches its most fully symbolic propor-tions. Though the political and personal questions remain important, in Macbeth's experience we come to see killing the king as a dramatic correlative for the thrust of anarchies of every kind against authority both external and internal. We never learn from precisely where the evil will to regicide reached Macbeth, but we follow in great detail what happens when a man violates a mode of traditional authority that turns out to be, in fact, an aspect of his own moral and spiritual health, thereby extinguishing in himself not merely the reality but even the dream of such a unity between microcosm and macrocosm as the old, nostalgic vision proposed.

One word will describe the process Macbeth undergoes: imprison-ment. This is the interior punishment exacted by his political crime. Having lost Duncan, the trusting king who allowed freedom and growth to all, Scotland becomes slave to the tyrant rebel who attri-butes his own motives to all, trusts no one therefore, and brings only death to his country. The personal story of Macbeth runs parallel. Having rejected all the traditional bonds which ordered life, however imperfectly (they did not keep Cawdor from rebelling, but did help defeat him), he becomes a slave to the narrow view of man and man's priorities held by his wife and by a part of himself. He becomes im-prisoned in the tyrannical authority of his own unrestricted egotism or self-will.

This is a profound psychological insight, as is Shakespeare's aware-ness that once such internal tyranny of self-will is established, it can-not easily be broken from within. Man cannot alone save himself from damnation; help must come from without—as his romances will show:

> And my ending is despair
> Unless I be reliev'd by prayer.   (*The Tempest,* Epilogue, 15-16)

In the terms of tragedy, the tyrant hero must be cut down for the good of the world at large. Though this is a loss, anything else would be worse. Furthermore, all of the resistances to regicide which he en-countered, even as he overrode them, would appear to have been only the fantastical visions of a deranged mind if he were not in turn to be attacked. Macduff's final act of regicide—so far as we know, the last in Shakespeare's works—confirms in a harsh, unflinching way the true existence of all those values and forces whose importance is proved negatively in the career of diminution and imprisonment that follows Macbeth's attempt to ignore them.

Killing the king gradually becomes then, in Shakespeare, a kind of lens in which all manner of political, social, moral, psychological, metaphysical, and religious questions are focused. What was perhaps implicit in the act in *Richard II* takes on explicit dramatic substance in *Macbeth*.

The Language of *Macbeth*

by Lawrence Danson

The Weird Sisters use a trick that would hardly have been news for the Delphic Oracle: through slight dislocations of normal grammatical or logical relationships, they make simple, even banal, statements sound as difficult as possible. That first portentous question, for instance, "When shall we three meet again?/ In thunder, lightning, or in rain?" turns out to be more a phatic than a fatidic utterance when once we reflect that, in all probability, they will have to meet in thunder, lightning, *and* in rain. Similarly, the answer, "When the battle's lost and won," sounds, at first, deeply paradoxical; but the paradox is immediately unraveled, the implicit riddle solved, when we realize that every battle is both lost and won: the Weird Sisters, unlike a mortal audience, are simply not engaged on any particular side.

True, the riddle has still a further dimension, for there is a sense in which Macbeth's temporary victory—the satisfaction of his desires—will prove to be his ultimate loss: but, again, it is a comprehensible statement which leaves the "rule in unity" unimpaired. The possibility of real inversions are contained in the Weird Sisters' rhetoric, inversions that would prove the triumph of disorder, unreality, and evil over their opposites; but with each such possibility there coexists the possibility that the inversions are merely apparent and that a reasonable order, the order of normal good, remains only partially and temporarily obscured.

These first two instances of fiendish paltering prepare us for that curious statement, "Fair is foul, and foul is fair." Again, it is a statement with a "double sense," one of which is paradoxical and extraordinary, another simple and reasonable. As a metaphysical statement, "Fair is foul, and foul is fair," carries us beyond the normal limits of logical thought: if the values "fair" and "foul" have really been reversed, and the things to which the words refer have really lost their identities, then the only languages in which they can be spoken of is the language of paradox. But the statement may not be metaphysical at all; the reversal may be only a matter of nomenclature which leaves the absolute values of "fair" and "foul" unaffected. In that case, the statement is merely metalinguistic, and the problem the Weird Sisters raise (which now may be paraphrased, "That which has been called 'fair' will now be called 'foul'") may conceivably be solved, not with the destruction of the rational universe, but with the revelation of the true order of things and the reimposition of a language actually descriptive of it.

Of course there is no way of determining, simply on the basis of the Weird Sisters' formulation, which interpretation is correct: it is entirely to the point that both interpretations have to be entertained simultaneously. For the riddle "Fair is foul, and foul is fair," is, in miniature, the riddle of the play itself. The entire action of *Macbeth* similarly hovers between a metaphysical horror and a metalinguistic mistake: Has the order of Nature really been destroyed by Macbeth, so that "nothing is but what is not"? Or do "measure, time, and place" (those certainties to which Malcolm will appeal in the final speech) still encompass and control the apparent perversion of Macbeth's reign? Has the fantastic Scotland of Macbeth's ascendancy, where relations are inverted until "to do harm/ Is often laudable, to do good sometime/ Accounted dangerous folly" (IV. ii. 74), become the image of some new metaphysical reality? Or will it prove merely a phantasm temporarily disguising the normal nature of Nature and "grace of Grace"?

In this *Macbeth*-world of apparently inherent ambiguity, the one perfectly unambiguous thing is the murder of Duncan. From the start it is conceived as just that: not sacrifice or revenge, but murder. We know from the start that the moral horror which is Duncan's murder cries out for retribution. Hence it is the murderer Macbeth's destiny that we most expectantly attend, and hence (in part) the unrelieved sense of inevitability and directness which gives *Macbeth* its distinctive dramatic concentration. And there is another cause, too, for this sense of concentration: in no other play does language so intimately and immediately reflect the action. Language in *Macbeth* is the mirror and even, in a sense, the cause of the extremity of the moral situation. Macbeth's deed is an overturning of normal values and relationships, and the language of the play (the Weird Sisters' speeches being only the most obvious examples) follows the action into the chaotic world he establishes, into the realm of impossibility, beyond the powers of ordinary conception, beyond the proper sphere of words.

Chronology of Important Dates

	Shakespeare	The Age
1558		Accession of Queen Elizabeth I.
1564	Shakespeare born at Stratford-upon-Avon: christened April 26th.	Christopher Marlowe born. Galileo born.
1570		Elizabeth excommunicated by Pope Pius V.
1577-80		Drake's voyage around the world.
1582	Shakespeare marries Anne Hathaway (license issued 27 November).	
1583	Shakespeare's daughter Susanna born (christened 26 May; died 1649).	
1584		Sir Walter Raleigh's attempts to colonize Virginia fail (1584-86).
1585	Shakespeare's twin son and daughter, Hamnet and Judith born (christened 2 February. Hamnet died 1596; Judith died 1662).	
1587		Mary Queen of Scots executed (8 February).
1588-89	Shakespeare's early plays begin to be performed in London.	Spanish Armada defeated (31 July-8 August, 1588).
1593	*Venus and Adonis* published.	Death of Marlowe.
1597		James VI, *Demonologie*.

Shakespeare	*The Age*
1598-99	*The Theatre* in Shoreditch torn down (December 1598); its timbers used to construct *The Globe* on Bankside (opened 1599). James VI, *Basilikon Doron* (1599). Death of Edmund Spenser (1599).
1600-01	*Hamlet* (published 1604: "bad" quarto, 1603).	
1603		Death of Queen Elizabeth I (24 March: her funeral 28 April). Accession of James VI as James I.
1605-06	*King Lear* (published 1608); *Macbeth* (published 1623).	Gunpowder Plot discovered (5 November 1605). Henry Garnet, Principal of the Jesuits, executed (1606).
1607	*Antony and Cleopatra* (1606-1607; published 1623).	Captain John Smith settles Jamestown, Virginia. The Irish earls, Tyrone and Tyroconnel, flee to the Continent.
1611-12	*The Tempest* (published 1623). Shakespeare retires to Stratford?	"Plantation" of Ulster underway.
1613		*The Globe* destroyed by fire.
1614		*The Globe* reopens on 30 June (demolished 1644).
1616	Shakespeare dies at Stratford, 23 April (buried 25 April).	Death of Cervantes.
1620		Pilgrims land at Plymouth Rock.
1623	First Folio edition of Shakespeare's plays published.	

Notes on the Editor and Contributors

TERENCE HAWKES, editor of this volume, is Senior Lecturer in English at University College, Cardiff. He is the author of *Shakespeare and the Reason, Shakespeare's Talking Animals,* and *Metaphor.* He is also the editor of *Coleridge on Shakespeare.*

CLEANTH BROOKS is Gray Professor of Rhetoric, Emeritus, at Yale University. One of the best-known of the "New Critics," he edited *The Southern Review* from 1935-1942 with Robert Penn Warren, and wrote the influential *Understanding Poetry* with him. His other works include *Modern Poetry and the Tradition* and (with W. K. Wimsatt) *A Short History of Literary Criticism.*

O. J. CAMBELL (1879-1970) was Professor of English at Columbia University. He was the author of *Comicall Satyre and Shakespeare's* Troilus and Cressida, and *Shakespeare's Satire* as well as co-editor of *The Reader's Encyclopedia of Shakespeare.*

R. S. CRANE (1886-1967), an influential member of the Chicago "Aristotelian" group of critics, was Distinguished Service Professor of English at the University of Chicago. In addition to *The Languages of Criticism and the Structure of Poetry,* he has written many authoritative essays and acted as editor of the volume *Critics and Criticism: Ancient and Modern.*

W. C. CURRY was Professor of English at Vanderbilt University. His published work includes studies of Chaucer and medieval science, and of Milton's cosmology.

LAWRENCE DANSON is an Assistant Professor of English at Princeton University.

G. R. ELLIOTT was formerly Folger Professor of English at Amherst College. He is well-known for his studies of *Hamlet (Scourge and Minister)* and *Othello (Flaming Minister),* as well as for his work on *Macbeth.*

D. J. ENRIGHT, novelist, poet, and critic, has lectured widely at universities in Egypt, Japan, and Malaysia. He was co-editor of *Encounter* from 1970-1972, and is currently a director of a London publishing house. In addition to *Shakespeare and the Students* he has written volumes of criticism called *The Apothecary's Shop* and *Conspirators and Poets.*

WILLARD FARNHAM, formerly Professor of English at the University of California, is author of *The Medieval Heritage of Elizabethan Tragedy,* as well as of numerous articles on Shakespeare and drama.

FRANCIS FERGUSSON was Professor of Comparative Literature at Rutgers University, and has taught at a number of other institutions, including the Institute for Advanced Studies at Princeton. His *The Idea of a Theater* has had considerable influence, and he is also well-known for his later *Dante's Drama of the Mind* and *The Human Image in Dramatic Literature.*

DAME HELEN GARDNER is Merton Professor of English Literature, Emeritus, at tne University of Oxford, and Fellow of Lady Margaret Hall. Among her many publications are *The Art of T. S. Eliot* and *A Reading of Paradise Lost;* she is also editor of *The Divine Poems of John Donne* and *The Oxford Book of English Verse.*

JOHN HOLLOWAY is Professor of Modern English Literature at Cambridge University. He is the author of many critical works including *The Victorian Sage, The Charted Mirror,* and *The Colours of Clarity.*

L. C. KNIGHTS was formerly King Edward VII professor of English Literature at Cambridge University. His publications include *Drama and Society in the Age of Jonson, Some Shakespearean Themes,* and *An Approach to Hamlet.*

MAYNARD MACK, JR. is Associate Professor of English at the University of Maryland.

MARY McCARTHY, novelist and journalist, was theater critic for *Partisan Review* from 1937 to 1957.

J. MIDDLETON MURRY (1889-1957), scholar and critic, was editor of the journals *Athenaeum* and *Adelphi.* His contributions to Shakespearean criticism include *Keats and Shakespeare,* and some essays in *Countries of the Mind* (2 vols.) as well as the volume *Shakespeare.*

A. P. ROSSITER (1905-1957) lectured at the University of Durham and at Cambridge University. He was the author of *English Drama from Earliest Times to the Elizabethans,* and editor of *Woodstock, a Moral History. Angel With Horns* was published posthumously.

CAROLINE SPURGEON (1869-1942) was Professor of English in the University of London. In addition to her work on Shakespeare's imagery, she edited a volume of Keats' annotations of Shakespeare.

EUGENE M. WAITH is Professor of English at Yale University and author of books and articles on English drama, including *The Pattern of Tragicomedy in Beaumont and Fletcher* and an edition of *Macbeth* (Yale Shakespeare).

ROY WALKER has written a study of *Hamlet* called *The Time Is Out of Joint* in addition to his study of *Macbeth.* He is also the author of *The Golden Feast: A Perennial Theme in Poetry.*

Selected Bibliography

Blissett, William, "The Secret'st Man of Blood: A Study of Dramatic Irony in *Macbeth," Shakespeare Quarterly,* 10 (1959), 397-408. This is an incisive account of a major aspect of the play.

Bradley, A. C. *Shakespearean Tragedy.* London: Macmillan, 1904. At his best, Bradley must rank as one of the great formative critics of Shakespeare. At his worst, the imposition of "literary" modes and preoccupations on the plays almost transforms them into second-rate novels. The essays on *Macbeth* in this volume have undeniable brilliance: but approach with caution.

Harcourt, John B. "I Pray You Remember the Porter," *Shakespeare Quarterly,* 12 (1961), 393-402. A good analysis of the Porter's crucial role.

Knight, G. Wilson. *The Wheel of Fire.* London: Oxford University Press, 1930; Methuen & Co., 1949 (rev. ed.). This influential volume contains a classic account of the play as a "vision of evil." Knight's subsequent study, *The Imperial Theme* (London: Oxford University Press, 1931) offers, in its essay "The Milk Of Concord," one of the finest "thematic" readings of the play available. The opposition it proposes between "life-themes" and "death-themes" has proved seminal.

Knights, L. C. *How Many Children Had Lady Macbeth?* Cambridge: The Minority Press, 1933; reprinted in *Explorations,* London: Chatto & Windus, 1946. A fundamental attack on Bradley's position, using *Macbeth* as evidence. This *locus classicus* of modern Shakespearean criticism involves a trenchant account of the play.

Paul, H. N. *The Royal Play of Macbeth,* New York: Macmillan, 1950. This is the standard work on the play's contemporary references.

Proser, Matthew N. *The Heroic Image in Five Shakespearean Tragedies.* Princeton, N.J.: Princeton University Press, 1965. This book offers a provocative development of the "manliness" discussion.

Ribner, Irving. *Patterns in Shakespearean Tragedy.* London: Methuen, 1960. Ribner sees *Macbeth* as "a closely knit, unified construction; every element of which supports a thematic statement."

Shakespeare Survey, 19 (1966). This issue is devoted entirely to *Macbeth* and contains several interesting items, particularly the essays by R. B. Heilman and W. A. Murry.

Stoll, E. E. *Art and Artifice in Shakespeare.* Cambridge: Cambridge University Press, 1933. Stoll's book attempts an interpretation of Shakespearean tragedy, including *Macbeth,* through Elizabethan eyes.